Unitarian Bibliography

Also from Westphalia Press

westphaliapress.org

The Idea of the Digital University

Masonic Tombstones and Masonic Secrets

Treasures of London

The History of Photography

L'Enfant and the Freemasons

Baronial Bedrooms

Making Trouble for Muslims

Material History and Ritual Objects

Paddle Your Own Canoe

Opportunity and Horatio Alger

Careers in the Face of Challenge

Bookplates of the Kings

Collecting American Presidential Autographs

Freemasonry in Old Buffalo

Original Cables from the Pearl Harbor Attack

Social Satire and the Modern Novel

The Essence of Harvard

The Genius of Freemasonry

A Definitive Commentary on Bookplates

James Martineau and Rebuilding Theology

No Bird Lacks Feathers

Earthworms, Horses, and Living Things

The Man Who Killed President Garfield

Anti-Masonry and the Murder of Morgan

Understanding Art

Homeopathy

Ancient Masonic Mysteries

Collecting Old Books

Masonic Secret Signs and Passwords

The Thomas Starr King Dispute

Earl Warren's Masonic Lodge

Lariats and Lassos

Mr. Garfield of Ohio

The Wisdom of Thomas Starr King

The French Foreign Legion

War in Syria

Naturism Comes to the United States

New Sources on Women and Freemasonry

Designing, Adapting, Strategizing in Online Education

Policy Diagnosis

Meeting Minutes of Naval Lodge No. 4 F.A.A.M

Unitarian Bibliography

H. McLachlan's
The Unitarian College Library

Introduced and Edited by Paul Rich

WESTPHALIA PRESS
An imprint of the Policy Studies Organization

Unitarian Bibliography
H. McLachlan's
The Unitarian College Library

Westphalia Press
An imprint of Policy Studies Organization
dgutierrezs@ipsonet.org

For information:
Westphalia Press
1527 New Hampshire Ave., N.W.
Washington, D.C. 20036

ISBN-13: 978-1935907251
ISBN-10: 1935907255

Updated material and comments on this edition can be found at the Westphalia Press website: westphaliapress.org

This edition is dedicated to the memory of
James Luther Adams,
distinguished in scholarship and in character.

Introduction to the New Edition

THE Unitarian College at Manchester in England was established in 1854, and it continues to this day. Currently it participates in a friendly consortium of theological colleges that share some facilities. It prepares ministers for the Unitarian churches in England and Scotland (and sometimes in Australia, New Zealand, and Canada) and for the Non-Subscribing Presbyterian Church of Ireland.

It also has played a role in hosting students for the Unitarian churches in Hungary and Rumania, where there are actually and surprisingly Unitarian bishops.

Confusingly, another college with Unitarian origins is Manchester Harris College in Oxford University. That institution also has collected Unitarian bibliography. And a third library, Dr. Williams Library in London, is another collector of Unitariana. All three institutions have played an important part in conserving the history of Nonconformist Britain.

This volume is a significant and permanent contribution to bibliography, with information that is available nowhere else. It is appropriate to dedicate this edition to the memory of Dr. Adams, whose influence on the Unitarian movement on both sides of the Atlantic was profound.

Paul Rich

E

F

THE UNITARIAN COLLEGE LIBRARY

Its History, Contents and Character

EXTERIOR OF LIBRARY

TO THE OLD STUDENTS

OF

THE UNITARIAN COLLEGE
MANCHESTER

Preface

IN a volume of Historical Essays, published in 1923 when the new Library was opened, a few pages sufficed for a brief sketch of its history, contents and character. The larger treatment of the subject here presented is due to more intimate acquaintance with it, to the growth of the Library, and, in particular, to the desire to impress on those who shall hereafter be responsible for its oversight the need for vigilance in its conduct and care.

The present international situation is the reason for the appearance of this volume earlier than had been intended, since delay might mean greatly increased cost of production.

Warm thanks are due, and are hereby tendered, to Mr. Ernest Axon F.S.A. for his careful reading of the proofs.

It is hoped that the story of the Library may increase interest in it, both in respect of its use and its patronage.

H. McLachlan

Manchester, September 21, 1939

CONTENTS

INTERIOR OF LIBRARY

THE UNITARIAN COLLEGE LIBRARY

I—Its History

HE history of the Unitarian College Library has in it little of romance and even less of ancient lore. It was founded by no medieval ecclesiastic or modern plutocrat, and only within living memory has attained to the slightest distinction amongst English libraries. Like the College itself, it had a humble origin, and its story is little more than a record of benefactions from private persons and chapel libraries, varied by purchases from grants provided by the College and other funds. That Unitarians, early and late, have been book-lovers, and that their chapels in former days gathered valuable collections, is manifest from the number and character of these donations.

Most of the laymen and ministers, whose books have found their way into the Library during the last eighty years, were men of culture and literary taste, and, what is equally important, they inherited or acquired their books long before agents of American collectors, with almost unlimited means, began the process of shipping rare volumes of every description across the Atlantic. Take e.g. the catalogue of the library of Thomas Henry Robinson, a Manchester merchant and a lay-student of Warrington Academy, who died in 1821, and that of the library of Rev. Robert Brook Aspland M.A., one time Secretary of Manchester College, who died in 1869. The ministerial collection numbered 5,500 volumes, including many rarities from the sixteenth, seventeenth and eighteenth centuries, some of which, bought by Unitarians, afterwards entered the Library. The lay collection numbered 2,906 volumes, many of which, bought by George William Wood, M.P., were later presented to the Library by his grandson.

Two manuscript letters afford first-hand accounts of ministerial book purchases in the first quarter of last century.

" I bought Ogilby's Virgil at Whateley's sale for £1. I bid £5 for his Aesop, which was pronounced to be a very fine copy by all the knowing ones present, but I had not the courage to go higher, so it was knocked down to my friend S. for £5 10s., and a very splendid small edition of Walpole's *Otranto* for 14s. 6d." (May 13, 1813.)

A layman, acting for a ministerial friend, indicates how an unscrupulous bookseller sometimes got the better of a purchaser whose instructions were not very precise.

" He says he was much inclined to secure all the Hebrew Bibles for you, as you marked the whole, and he thought you laid stress upon them. . . . On the whole, you will perceive it to be our opinion that you must take the lot. . . . Perhaps you would be kind enough to remit £100 and the balance I will adjust." (January 18, 1821.)

It is curious that more than once books from the same private collection have been brought together in the Library as the result of gifts at intervals of many years. Two examples will show what is meant.

John Pope (1745–1802) was the son of John Pope (1716–1785), originally a tailor and then a bookseller at Exeter, where he lived and died. John Pope Jr. was educated at the second Exeter Academy under Samuel Merivale, Micaijah Towgood and John Turner, was Minister at Blackley, nr. Manchester, 1767–1791, Tutor in Classics, Hackney College, 1791–1793, and again Minister at Blackley from 1793 until his death in 1802. During his second ministry at Blackley he was also Master at Stand Grammar School, and one of his pupils was Robert Smethurst (1778–1846), a native of Blackley, Minister at Monton, and for twenty-four years, 1798–1822, Master at Stand School. John Pope, a man of real classical scholarship,[1] was much esteemed by his contemporaries. Probably he inherited his love of books from his father, and possibly some of the volumes in his library had been originally acquired by the Exeter bookseller. Apparently Pope's collection was broken up on his death, for Robert Smethurst purchased some volumes, which, on his own death in 1846, passed into the possession of the Rev. John Colston M.A., of Styal, and formed part of his bequest to the Library in 1878. Other books from the same library were acquired on Pope's death by Robert Philips Esq., of The Park, Prestwich, whose connection with Stand Chapel went back to the eighteenth century, and eventually came to Summerville in 1933 by donation from the present representative of the Philips family.[2] Again, many of the books collected by the Rev. John Ralph, Minister at Halifax 1767–1795, were presented to the College in its earliest days by his daughter, whilst others, which he had given to the Northgate End Chapel Library, were presented by the chapel to the Library in 1938.

The active interest of laymen in social, political and educa-

---

[1] See pp. 104-5.   [2] See pp. 30-31.

tional reform is reflected in their gifts to the Library, which have imparted to it a character more comprehensive than is commonly the mark of a theological library.

Ministers not only assembled books for themselves; they were also prominent amongst the founders of subscription libraries throughout the country, *e.g.* John Seddon, at Warrington, 1758; Joseph Priestley, at Leeds, 1770; John Dean, at Bradford, 1774; Thomas Watson, at Whitby, 1775; and Charles Wellbeloved, at York, 1794. These instances might be multiplied.

Chapel libraries, many of them founded in the eighteenth century, were the rule not the exception amongst Unitarians. These in the first instance were mainly though not exclusively theological, and often rich in the literature of Dissent. To name only a few from which, amongst others, the Unitarian College Library has benefited: —The library at Newcastle-upon-Tyne was founded by William Turner in 1757. In the preface to the catalogue published in 1809, he remarks: " Most of the treatises which have been published in our own, or translated out of other languages, upon the Evidences, Principles and Duties of Natural and Revealed Religion; the grounds of our separation from Popery, and our Dissent from the Church of England . . . many judicious illustrations of Scripture doctrine and Precepts, explanations of Scripture difficulties, and accounts of most of the distinguished sects and persuasions into which the Christian world has been divided. Particularly the reader will find himself furnished with a pretty complete history of the state of religion in this island, and especially of those public transactions which more immediately concerned the Dissenters." The catalogue includes 764 volumes, folio, quarto and octavo from the seventeenth and eighteenth centuries. The library at Bank Street Chapel, Bolton, was founded in 1789 by John Holland, nephew and successor of Philip Holland,[1] one of the founders of Warrington Academy, who had himself left a large number of books to the chapel. In 1854 the library consisted of 1,500 volumes, many of them " scarce works connected with Dissent." Joseph Priestley founded the library at Gravel Pit, Hackney, during his ministry there, 1791–1794. The catalogue includes 570 volumes. At Shrewsbury, the library, founded in the eighteenth century, in 1847, numbered 600 volumes. Cross Street Chapel Library, Manchester, another eighteenth century foundation, in 1884, included more than 2,000 volumes, many of them quite rare, and additions were made for at least thirty years.

[1] For an account of Philip Holland, founder of the Widows' Fund Association (1764), see the *Widows' Fund Association*, pp. 20-21, by the writer.

Libraries founded in the eighteenth and early nineteenth century often contained ministerial collections from a much earlier date, *e.g.* the Stourbridge Chapel Library contained volumes from the library of the Rev. John Toncks, 1687-1757. A few chapel libraries were handed over to the local authorities after the passing of the Free Libraries Act of 1850. Chowbent Chapel Library, founded as a book club in 1761, survived until 1905, when the collection of 4,000 volumes was presented to the recently erected Carnegie Free Library in the town.

Some degenerated into Sunday School libraries. Bank Street Chapel Library, Bury, established in 1804, following a much earlier book club, boasted in 1858 that it was " as complete as any," but subsequently, after gifts to the chapel at Heywood, became a school library. Occasionally, chapels possessed books long before a library was formally established. " At Knutsford," says the Rev. G. A. Payne,[1] " the library was opened in 1830, but four volumes of Baxter's works were given on September 23, 1730, by a merchant of London to the congregation."[2]

Not a few chapel libraries were dispersed by careless or impecunious custodians. Amongst these was that of Bowl Alley Lane, Hull. It was founded by the bequest of Leonard Chamberlain in 1716, and included " Walton's Polyglott Bible, Trostius' Syriac New Testament, the works of many of the Greek and Latin Fathers, the Mattaire Classics, several good editions of Horace, Juvenal, Cicero, etc., together with Camden's Britannia, Thoresby's Leeds and other historical works." Later, larger additions were made to the collection of modern publications, and in 1818 the library was said to have been " much used." It was dispersed in 1883, after the removal of the congregation to Park Street. A few chapel libraries still survive, amongst the most important being those of Liverpool (Ullet Road, and Hope Street), Birmingham (Church of the Messiah), Leeds, Belfast 1st Congregation and Dublin.

The erection of public libraries, together with the advent of the cheap Press and circulating libraries, the decline of interest in theological controversy and the complete tolerance of Dissent led to the disuse of chapel libraries, and, subsequently, to their transference, in whole or in part, to the College, especially after it possessed a hall of residence and a suitable library building of its own.

To the first printed catalogue of an early Manchester chapel library at Mosley Street, afterwards Upper Brook Street, " directions are prefixed, marking out a course of connected reading furnished by the volumes it contained," and

[1] An Ancient Chapel, p. 30.   [2] Ibid, p. 70.

the library was designed, it is said, " for a class who, with limited means and leisure, are honourably distinguished by a love of mental culture and by a deep and intelligent interest in religious questions." As already stated, the College Library contains many volumes formerly in the possession of the Rev. John Ralph, Minister of Northgate End Chapel, Halifax, 1767–1795. Ralph, whose daughter was the mother of Sir James Stansfeld, the radical statesman, was an ancestor of the late Professor Courtney Kenny, of Cambridge, and the founder of the chapel library at Halifax. The library in 1862 numbered 644 volumes. The spirit of the man is reflected in the nature of that foundation. " It is proposed to collect a small library of books calculated to promote religious knowledge, and principally such as illustrate the truths and enforce the doctrines of Christianity. As it behoveth us *to try all things,* it is not intended to exclude the writers upon any doctrinal system, provided their books breathe the spirit of that religion they are designed to teach." This spirit of toleration and free but reverent enquiry seems to have animated the founders of libraries whose books in process of time have helped so materially to build up the College Library. This is especially fitting, since the Library is part of an institution which, in the words of the preamble to its constitution, " adheres to the principle of freely imparting theological knowledge without insisting on the adoption of any particular theological doctrine." We may rightly regard the College Library as, in a sense, the residuary legatee of those spiritual values, dependent for expression upon intellectual culture, formerly guarded by our old chapels.

Until 1922 the Library never enjoyed any endowment. Consequently, this most necessary aid to education in a theological college has occasionally suffered neglect, and its claims have been subordinated to other and more urgent demands.

It is impossible to trace in detail the growth of the collection, but, of the donations, a few of the earlier, the larger, more interesting and valuable deserve to be recorded.

At the outset the College provided neither lecture-room nor library for its students. Established May 31, 1854, as the Unitarian Home Missionary Board, for a few months its classes were held at the residences of its tutors, the Rev. J. R. Beard D.D. and the Rev. William Gaskell M.A. in Lower Broughton and Plymouth Grove respectively. From August, 1855, for a year, three rooms were occupied at 102 Cross Street. Subsequently lectures were given in the chapel room attached to Cross Street Chapel. Here students had the use of the chapel

B

library. In addition, they had access to Chetham's Library (founded 1656), which claims to be the oldest free library in England, to which their predecessors in the first and second Manchester Academies, established 1699 and 1786, had resorted, and also to the Manchester Free Library (established 1852), then housed in Campfield in the building erected as a Hall of Science by the disciples of Robert Owen. In 1856 the Board found a home, if the euphemism may pass, in four rooms at the top of an old warehouse in 8 Marsden Square, where the nucleus of a library was formed by a grant (£55 4s.) from funds raised by subscribers to the Board and by the gifts of a number of friends. The Principal was requested to act as curator of the Library and to appoint a student as his assistant with an honorarium of two guineas a year. In 1858 a gift of books and manuscripts was acknowledged from the library of the Rev. J. G. Robberds (1789–1854), for over forty years Minister of Cross Street Chapel, Professor of Hebrew and Syriac, 1840–1845, and of Pastoral Theology, 1840–1852, at Manchester New College. James Heywood Esq., M.A., M.P., the second President of the Board, who laid the foundations of the Owens College Library with a gift of 1,200 books in 1851, seven years later presented the Library with 240 volumes and with many others in 1860. The name of John Colston, whose portrait hangs in the present Library, first appears as a patron in the same year. An old student of Manchester New College, Minister of Styal, 1833–1863, and tutor in the family of Robert Hyde Greg, Colston was a man of considerable scholarship and a most generous benefactor of the Library, to which at his death in 1878 he bequeathed an extensive collection, including valuable editions of the New Testament, folio and quarto, and many rare theological works. Cross Street Chapel Library was the first of many such libraries to increase the College collection, adding thirty-four volumes in 1858 and 223 volumes in the following year. In 1861 the institution had amassed such wealth that it was deemed prudent to insure its property in books, and a policy was taken out for £100!

The celebration of the bicentenary of " the ejected of 1662 " led to the erection by Unitarians of the Memorial Hall in Albert Square (opened January 18, 1866), the first hall built in Manchester by any religious body. Here the College with its Library was housed for thirty-nine years.

Testimony to the good feeling between the *alumni* of two kindred institutions was borne by the presentation to the Library in 1866 of the facsimile of *Codex Sinaiticus*, then lately published, by some of the old students of Manchester New College, which had acquired a copy by gift from the Czar of Russia, the patron of Tischendorf, who discovered the famous manuscript now in the British Museum. Next year, Miss Jane Ellen Yates, of Liverpool, an early and generous supporter of the College, presented 300 books from the library of her father, the Rev. John Yates (1755–1826), an old student of Warrington Academy.

In 1867 also, Mr. Henry Arthur Bright M.A., afterwards (1873) President of the Board, gave two bound volumes of the MS. letters of Theophilus Lindsey (1723–1808), addressed to William Tayleur, of Shrewsbury, a Cambridge graduate, friend and patron of Joseph Priestley. According to Bright, writing August 11, 1877, the letters had "formerly belonged to his uncle, Benjamin Heywood Bright, an eminent book collector and Shakesperian critic," and he expressed his "wonder that no student of the Home Missionary Board had found time or inclination to compile extracts from the more important letters which had more than a denominational value." In 1920 they were used, with other letters, in a volume published by the Manchester University Press. Whilst engaged upon these letters, the writer discovered in a Birmingham bookseller's shop the replies to them by Tayleur, which were purchased for the Library. In March, 1924, thanks to the good offices of Mr. J. P. Gibson, Keeper of MSS. in the British Museum, the co-operation of the Rev. J. A. Pearson and the generosity of the late Mr. T. B. Taylor, of London, the College acquired a third volume of MS. letters of Lindsey to Tayleur, which originally formed part of the collection in the possession of Henry A. Bright. At the request of the latter, this volume, mainly political in character, had been presented, July, 1884, shortly after his death, to the late Right Hon. Charles G. Milnes-Gaskell, upon whose decease it passed into a London auction room.

Amongst numerous volumes presented in 1867 by the Rev. R. L. Carpenter M.A. was a fine set of eighteenth-century tracts and pamphlets, originally in the library of Dr. Lant Carpenter (1780–1840), and the folio volumes of the *Bibliotheca Fratrum Polonorum quos Unitarios Vocant* (1656).

In 1870 the Library was reorganised, and a catalogue prepared by Mr. John Chadwick (1833–1918), for long connected with Mudie's Library. He had assisted in putting the books on the shelves of Owens College in Quay Street in 1852, was present at the meeting in Cross Street Chapel Room in 1854 when the Unitarian College was founded and listened to a lecture at Summerville in 1914 on its sixtieth anniversary. Mr. T. P. Jones, caretaker of the Memorial Hall, was appointed librarian at a salary of £5 a year. Permission to use the Library was granted to former students and to members of the local Lay-Preachers' Union. Amongst donors of books this year were the executors of Samuel Alcock, one of the first trustees of Owens College. In 1872 some photograph copies of ancient manuscripts of the New Testament, with annotations by Dr. J. G. Greenwood, the second Principal of Owens College, were framed and presented anonymously to the Library by the Rev. Brooke Herford.

From 1872 the minutes of the Library Committee have been preserved. The first chairman was Dr. H. J. Marcus (1811–1885), a native of Mecklenburg, Honorary Professor of German in the College, and the first secretary was the Rev. T. E. Poynting (1813–1879), its tutor in theology. Books required for their use by students were purchased, and a grant of books, mainly American, made by the British and Foreign Unitarian Association. In 1873, £20 was voted to the Library by the committee of the institution, £10 in the following year and other similar small sums at intervals later. The librarian in his report for 1873 mentioned by name the students who had made use of the Library, and those, three in number, who had found no use for it. He also observed that no book with an old cover had any chance of being read. At this date, the Library contained 1,585 volumes. In 1874 the Library purchased at a nominal sum (£5) from Manchester New College a number of duplicates of theological, philosophical and biographical works. These included scarce volumes, some of which had formerly been in the libraries of a few of the old academies. During the year £14 10s. had been spent on the Library, and amongst the gifts to it were seventy-one volumes from Mr. Henry Turner, of which fifty-four were from the eighteenth and two from the seventeenth century.

In 1875 a special grant of £10 was voted by the Board for the purpose of drawing up a complete manuscript catalogue of the Library. The work was entrusted to the capable hands of Mr. (afterwards Dr.) W. E. A. Axon, the well-known antiquary, who received the degree of M.A. *honoris causa* from Manchester University in 1913. It was completed in the course of twelve months, and afforded the compiler materials for an article in his *Lancashire Gleanings* (1883) upon a rare sixteenth century sermon.

Amongst the gifts received during this period were a hundred volumes from the library of Dr. J. R. Beard, the late Principal, and many volumes from the collections of the late Rev. Henry Green M.A., formerly Visitor of the Board, and of the late Rev. T. E. Poynting, its former tutor in theology.

In his *Handbook of the Public Libraries of Manchester and Salford* (1877), W. E. A. Axon gives three pages to the Library. He observes that it is " very small," the sections devoted to general literature are very unimportant," " the classics few in number " and that " the library possesses only one manuscript." He adds that " of works relating to the Racovian controversy there is a much finer collection in the Free Library," and gives the number of volumes in the Unitarian Library as " about 3,000."

In 1878 it was reported by the Library Committee that more than 800 volumes had been added since the MS. catalogue had been made two years earlier. In 1879 reports of the British Association for 1855–1868 were presented by the Rev. A. W. Worthington, Mr. H. Leigh added a few and Mr. G. W. Rayner Wood brought the set up to date, and continued to present each report as it appeared until his death in 1926. In 1878, also, a number of valuable books, folio and quarto, were given by the Rev. G. H. Wells M.A., of Gorton. In 1881 Dr. R. C. Christie, Chancellor of the Diocese and formerly Professor at Owens College, gave a number of theological books and pamphlets, including some used in the preparation of his *Etienne Dolet The Martyr of the Renascence,* published in 1880. These included *Interpretationes Paradoxae Quatuor Evangelorum* (1674) by Christopher Sandius, described by the donor as " a learned book and not easily met with."

The task of cataloguing the Library afresh, with the help of the manuscript slips prepared by Axon, was now undertaken by the Revs. James Black and J. E. Odgers, tutors of the Board. It was finished and 500 copies printed in 1882 at a cost of £22. Copies were presented to tutors and students and the rest offered for sale (6d. each). At this date the Library numbered 3,621 volumes, exclusive of unbound sermons and pamphlets. Its poverty is apparent from a letter of Principal Odgers written at this time, appealing for donations.

" Beginning a course on Anti-Trinitarian opinions," he said, " there is nothing to which I can refer my students. We have no *origines* but *Fratres Poloni*; we have neither such modern books as those of Trechsel, Fock, Benrath, Tollin, or such histories as those of Sandius, Bock, Maimburg, Lamy. We have nothing about Servetus, we have no confessions or symbolical books, but Rees's *Racovian Catechism*; we have not a set of the old *Unitarian Tracts*; we have not even Toulmin's *View of Dissenters* or Lindsey's *View of Unitarian Doctrine.*"

Amongst the donors in 1883 were Miss Wallace, from the

library of her father, the Rev. Robert Wallace (1790–1850), Professor of Critical Theology at Manchester New College, and Mr. John Fretwell. The last named, a zealous promoter of international relations between the Unitarians of England, America, Hungary and the German liberal religious thinkers, presented several rare seventeenth century works purchased by him in Germany. In October, 1884, the Rev. J. H. Bibby, of Ballee, made his first gift to the Library, consisting of twenty-four volumes purchased from the library of the late Rev. John Porter (1801–1874), Minister of the Second Presbyterian Church, Belfast, 1829–1870. It was the first of a long succession of gifts from old students and their families. Chiefly from collections of books by old Presbyterian divines in Ireland, Mr. Bibby built up his own library from which he made a large donation in 1931 and bequeathed the rest three years later to the College. In 1885, over fifty volumes were given by the family of the late Rev. W. C. Squier, of Stand, one of the first students of the College, including a handsome edition of the works of Lardner which he had won as a prize whilst a student. The Rev. J. E. Carpenter M.A. gave seventy volumes, many being books presented to him by the Hibbert Trustees, and, responding to the call of Principal Odgers, included a set of the old *Unitarian Tracts.*

In 1883, in consequence of the retirement through ill-health of Mr. T. P. Jones from the office of keeper of the Memorial Hall, he resigned his post as librarian. Principal Odgers was appointed to fill the vacancy, and a student, Mr. J. H. Weatherall, later Principal of Manchester College, Oxford, became his assistant.

An almost complete set of the two series of the Chetham Society publications was presented this year by Mr. Samuel Fielden, of Todmorden, " on a promise to continue the subscription " after his death, a condition in which the Committee cheerfully acquiesced but did not fulfil until 1917, when their attention was drawn to it by Professor James Tait, then President of the Society. In 1888, a number of books were added from the Hope Street Chapel Library, Liverpool, and from the library of the late Rev. Richard Pilcher B.A.

In 1890 the Rev. Alexander Gordon M.A., the new Principal of the College, as it was henceforth called, was appointed librarian. Gordon examined and reported on the Library, observing that " it was more valuable than he expected to find it." Its value was quickly increased by the bequest of a collection of books by Henry James Morehouse F.S.A. (1804–1890), Surgeon, of Lydgate, near Huddersfield. The family of

Morehouse was one of the oldest in the district, the name appearing as far back as the reign of Richard II, and from the time of Queen Elizabeth their property, Stoney Bank, near Holmfirth, had descended in unbroken succession from father to son. Morehouse was one of the founders of the Yorkshire Archaeological Association, a Fellow of the Society of Antiquaries, and the author of the *History of Kirkburton, and of the Graveship of Holme*. He had an accurate knowledge of the old Presbyterian congregations, and, through his ancestors, was connected with the leaders of Yorkshire Nonconformity of 200 years ago.[1] The books which came into the College Library included many scarce theological works of the seventeenth century that had formerly belonged, as their inscriptions show, to the ancestors of Mr. Morehouse, the last of his line. Many interesting notes, biographical and bibliographical, are written on the fly-leaves of these books by their late owner. Some of these will be discussed later.

A sum of £34, voted by the Trustees of the Gaskell Scholarship, added some modern books to the Library, but a report in September, 1892, declared that whilst rich in some departments, especially classics, it was poor in others, notably English literature, and betrayed great gaps in the history of Nonconformity. In 1896 a number of books were presented by Mr. J. J. Bradshaw, of Bolton, in memory of his father, John Bradshaw (1797–1858), and the following year sixty-three volumes were added from the library of Bank Street Chapel, Bolton, with which he had been long connected.

Amongst benefactors of the Library now and later were Professor Courtney Kenny, of Cambridge, and the Hibbert Trustees. In 1897 from the library of the late Rev. William Mitchell, an old student of the College, came many books, including bound pamphlets and some fifty volumes of articles from various quarterly magazines, arranged according to subject. In 1900 the Library was enriched by a handsome donation of philosophical and theological works from the library of the late Dr. Martineau. Sir Edwin Durning-Lawrence Bart., President of the College 1910–1913, ever a staunch friend, presented the Library in 1904 with the ninth edition of the *Encyclopaedia Britannica,* and the *Dictionary of National Biography,* and a little later with the Macklin Bible, in six folio volumes, and the eleventh edition of the *Encyclopaedia Britannica.* In 1910 he gave three precious volumes of the works of Servetus,[2] on the condition that should the College be discontinued or amalgamated with another institution they are to be transferred to the University of Edinburgh.

[1] For an account of the family of Morehouse see p. 91.   [2] See p. 51.

The jubilee of the College was celebrated in 1904 by raising a fund of over £20,000, and the purchase of a residential hall at Summerville, Victoria Park, opened October 12, 1905. The main part of the Library was housed in what are now lecture-room and chapel, a special collection in what was then the lecture-room and the rest accommodated in the common-room.

The movement of the Library from Albert Square to Victoria Park was momentous. The College rooms in the Memorial Hall had been occupied by various denominational societies and committees almost every week-day, afternoon and evening, and closed on Sunday. Consequently there was every inducement to students to seek elsewhere the books they wished to read. If the Register of Books Issued from 1882 to 1904 is trustworthy, it had become something of an event for students, after they became members of Owens College, to borrow books from their own Library. Borrowers, few in number, were mostly ministers and College tutors. In 1882, there are four entries of books taken out; ten years later, the number had risen to twenty; but in 1902 had fallen to seven. One student, assistant librarian 1899–1900, later a lecturer in the College, boasted that during his year of office he never saw the Library. The present writer borrowed three books in six years. The returning of books borrowed was a matter almost of caprice. Even the Principal, to say the least, was never in any hurry about it. In a letter, dated February 3, 1914, Alexander Gordon admitted that three volumes of Rutt's edition of Priestley's works and a folio (1615) of Aquinas, borrowed respectively, July 27, 1893, and July 16, 1898, were still in his possession. They were not recovered until after his death in 1931. The trio had been missing for thirty-eight years, the other for thirty-three. As the Principal at this period kept the record of books borrowed, until he resigned in 1911 no one could call his attention to his excessive attachment to Priestley and Aquinas. He must, however, be credited with the entry which enabled one to rescue them from a depository where they had lain undisturbed, clad in a thick mantle of dust, for nearly twenty years. Alas, some thirty books, which had disappeared, were seen no more, despite a courteous circular on the subject addressed to old students. The loaned and lost included one volume of the *Jewish Encyclopædia,* to the publication of which the College had subscribed, and another, of *Chambers Encyclopædia.* In course of time their places were filled by other copies.

From the settlement of the College at Summerville in 1905, the books came gradually into use, but necessarily only to a limited extent, for the volumes, scattered in three rooms and heaped together as in a poor second-hand bookseller's shop, were covered with the grime of years, many of them with backs broken and, for the more part, bearing no visible mark of identification. What was more, they were uncatalogued, and, as Thomas Carlyle once said: " A library is not worth anything without a catalogue; it is a Polyphemus without any eye in his head."

In January, 1904, it had been suggested that the approaching jubilee of the College would be a fitting occasion for the establishment of a Library Endowment Fund, but no action was taken. Exactly nine years later, the matter was raised again with the same result.

With the establishment this year of the Theological Faculty at Manchester University, several students began to read for the divinity degree, and a large number of text-books in all subjects taken were purchased.

From 1904 to 1910, the meetings of the Library Committee were suspended; all the energies of staff and committee being expended in the attempt to raise the Jubilee Fund of £20,000. Through the efforts of the Rev. John Moore, an album containing the portraits of the students of the College from 1854 was presented to the Library, and, amongst other gifts of this date, was a set of the *Delphin Classics* from the Rev. John Dale, another old student of the College.

In accordance with the will and codicil of the Rev. William Blazeby B.A., of Rotherham, his library, consisting of over 2,000 volumes and manuscripts, was bequeathed to the College in 1908, conditionally upon the books being placed in a suitable room, or in a separate apartment of a room, to be designated "The Blazeby Collection." The gift was accompanied by a legacy of £200. The collection is rich in history and biography, especially of the Stuart and Cromwellian periods. In 1909, the Rev. R. B. Drummond B.A., of Edinburgh, author of the *Life of Erasmus* (two vols. 1873), presented to the Library the *Works of Erasmus* (eleven vols. folio), and, at his death twelve years later, forty-four more volumes were received from his library.

In 1910, Mr. Gordon began to catalogue the Blazeby Collection on the Aberdeen sheaf system, but had only completed a third of the whole when in 1911 he resigned the principalship of the College. The present writer, appointed honorary librarian December 7, 1911, completed that catalogue, and began the work, finished in 1912, of cataloguing the whole library on the card system. This filthy but fascinating task enlisted the sympathy and co-operation of the students, who enjoyed what resembled in certain respects a voyage of discovery. Upon a petition being directed to the Gaskell Scholarship Trustees, a grant of £150 was made; £100 for new books and the balance for repairs and renovations. At the same time their annual grant was increased to £10. The effect of catalogue, renovation and additions was apparent in the increased use made of the Library—205 books being taken out in 1912, a number that steadily rose in succeeding years. In 1912, sixty-five volumes, including several folios, were given by the Rev. Charles Hargrove Litt.D., at whose death in 1917 fifty-three more came from the same collection, the larger part of which went to Leeds University.

In May, 1912, new Library rules were adopted, which provided *inter alia* that " *Alumni* of the College and neighbouring ministers may consult books in the Library, but not remove them except by permission of the librarian." In 1926, this permission was extended so as to include " University men provided with suitable introductions." A volume was also procured in which suggestions of books to be purchased could be recorded by students. Previously, all purchases had been made on the recommendation of members of the College staff or of the Library Committee.

In 1913, the Library Committee lost by death the services of the honorary secretary since 1900—the Rev. George Evans M.A., formerly Hibbert Fellow, in whose memory his daughter presented 220 of his books, amongst them many valuable Semitic works. The new secretary was the present Principal. On March 17, 1914, the Library Committee recommended that a separate Library account be included in the College annual report, and this first appeared in the report for 1915.

In addition to others specially named, chapel libraries which have donated books at different times are: —Dean Row, Cheshire; Hackney, London; Oldham; Hope Street, Liverpool; Strangeways and Upper Brook Street, Manchester; Tenterden; Upper Chapel, Sheffield; Hale, Cheshire; Birkenhead; Shrewsbury; Chowbent; Swansea; Newcastle-upon-Tyne; Davenport; Southampton; Hinckley; Wakefield; Padiham; Stourbridge; Evesham; Leeds. The British and Foreign Unitarian Association and Dr. Williams' Trust made grants of modern works. In 1913, Mr. P. J. Winser, lay-secretary of the College, presented the Library with a marble bust of the Rev. William Gaskell M.A., the second Principal, together with a chalk study of him by W. Percy and a number of books purchased at the sale of the Gaskell effects consequent on the death of

Miss Gaskell. Mr. Winser continued his patronage of the Library until his death in 1916, when his widow gave 233 valuable books from his collection.

In May, 1915, in response to the appeal of the librarian of the John Rylands Library for a gift of books towards a collection for the University of Louvain to replace that destroyed by the Germans during the Great War, fifty-eight volumes were presented by the Library, and acknowledged by Dr. Guppy as "most acceptable contributions." In all nearly 50,000 volumes were collected and sent to Louvain. The College donation had one happy result. Mr. George W. Rayner Wood J.P., a member of the College Committee, on hearing of it, invited the writer to go through his library with a view to selecting books for Louvain, and readily agreed to the suggestion that at the same time consideration should be given to the needs of the College Library. Subsequently, in October, 1915, 154 volumes were added to the Louvain collection, and the College received 459 books, most of which belonged to the seventeenth and eighteenth centuries. Five years later, Mr. Wood gave forty-two more, and, on his death in 1926, his widow added 250. Most of these volumes had been collected by his forbears: —William Wood (1745-1909), the successor of Joseph Priestley at Mill Hill Chapel, Leeds; George William Wood M.P., whose labours on behalf of the Dissenters' Chapels Act (1844) led to his premature death; and William Rayner Wood J.P. (1811-1884), one of the most prominent Unitarians of his day.

In 1915 also came some seventy volumes from Dr. Williams' library, the earliest and most important storehouse of Nonconformist literature.

George Thomas Esq., J.P., of Irlam Hall, not only for many years gave a large number of books, but also presented almost complete sets of the publications of the Manchester Literary Club and the Manchester Geographical Society, and paid two subscriptions for ten years to each society that students might enjoy their meetings and use their libraries—subscriptions that have been continued by the College. He also gave a long set of the *National Geographic Magazine* of New York on condition that after his death the Principal of the College should be made a member of the society. In 1922 he crowned his benefactions by a donation of 500 guineas as an Endowment Fund for the Library, which, with the grants of £10 a year from the Gaskell Scholarship, and, since 1915, an annual grant of the same sum from the Sharpe Hungarian Scholarship Fund, constitutes the main income of the Library, apart from special grants from the

Gaskell Scholarship Fund, whose accumulated reserves, according to the Trust, may only be spent on the Library. The income is spent on modern theological works, except that, in accordance with a resolution of the Library Committee in 1913, " Special attention is paid to the literature of Nonconformist (and especially Unitarian) history." In this way we remedy what has been called by a London librarian " the great defect of our smaller English libraries," viz. " their unsystematic collection of books." " Instead of building up strong special sections, they attempt to imitate on a feeble scale general libraries with large resources."

Many widows of old students, from time to time, have made substantial gifts to the Library from ministerial collections. Another pleasing type of gift, from 1913 on, has been provided by the students, who have invariably marked their appreciation of the help afforded them by the Library by adding one or more volumes, with their names and years, on leaving College to enter the ministry. In recent years, university research students using the Library have done the same.

Mr. F. W. Monks J.P., Vice-Chairman of Committee 1904–1913, Chairman 1914–1923, and President 1925–1929, was, until his death in 1932, a most generous patron of the Library. In the decade 1919–1929, he purchased and presented, at the suggestion of the Principal, 350 volumes and many rare manuscripts, which otherwise could not have been acquired. From 1920 to 1922, the late Mr. T. F. Wright, the great-grandson of a Unitarian minister, presented no fewer than a thousand volumes, most of which are standard editions of works in literature and biography. A pathetic interest attaches to these gifts, as for some years before his death the donor was totally deaf and blind. He knew, however, every volume by touch, and, from memory, their contents. He conversed by means of letters cut in cardboard, and in this way imparted information concerning his books.

In 1922, the British and Foreign Unitarian Association and the Sunday School Association placed the Library on the free list, and made grants of past publications. This has been continued by their successor, the General Assembly of Unitarian and Free Christian Churches. In the same year, the Gaskell Scholarship Trustees again marked their interest in the Library by a special grant of £200. Being thus enriched through the generosity of friends, the Library Committee deemed it not unfitting to raise the honorarium of the assistant librarian to £5.

On June 6, 1923, the new Library building was opened by Sir John Brunner Bart., The President of the College. Occupying the site of the old stables and coach-house, the Library was built from the plans of Mr. Norman F. Shanks A.R.I.B.A., son of an old student of the College. Amongst the speakers at the opening was Professor Tout, who in the course of his remarks said he " was proud to testify personally to the value of the Library. That the Library was such a vital thing was, of course, due to the fact that it had been shepherded by scholars. In certain directions the Library was unique, and he and his colleagues would avail themselves of the facilities offered to them and use the Library the more freely because it was so nobly housed."

A new typewritten card catalogue (authors and subject) was now made by the Principal on a more extensive plan than before, with numerous cross references, and completed within three years.

Shortly after the opening of the Library, the Cross Street Chapel Trustees handed over to it 668 volumes selected by the Principal. These included Walton's Polyglot, 1654–1657, formerly the property of Joseph Mottershead, minister of the chapel 1717–1771, numerous seventeenth century folios and quartos, and modern works " purchased for the Chapel Library out of the balance of the subscriptions for the memorial tablet placed in the Chapel " commemorating William Gaskell " who died June 11th, 1884, in the 79th year of his age and the 56th of his ministry in Cross Street Chapel." The same year, at the invitation of the Rev. Dr. Wilbur, President of the Pacific Unitarian School for the Ministry, U.S.A., a regular exchange of duplicates was arranged with the American college. Subsequently for several years a considerable number of modern American works found their way to Summerville, including *The Catholic Encyclopædia* (sixteen vols.), published 1907–1914. In 1924–1925, 154 volumes, mostly French, were presented by the Rev. A. E. O'Connor B.D., a graduate of Geneva University. In September, 1925, the Rev. Alexander Gordon gave 250 volumes, largely from the seventeenth and eighteenth centuries. A little later, books presented by the Rev. W. C. Bowie D.D., a former student, and for many years secretary of the British and Foreign Unitarian Association, included prizes won at Owens College and autographed copies of Unitarian works, English and American, presented to him by their authors. In 1926, the Rev. Philemon Moore B.A., another old student, Visitor of the College 1890–1917, late Professor of Hebrew and

Hellenistic Greek at Carmarthen College, presented seventy-eight volumes on New Testament criticism, and four years later bequeathed 371 volumes, chiefly on Semitic and Oriental literature.

In May, 1930, a number of books were purchased from the library of the late Professor A. S. Peake.

Gifts, other than books, at this time included a bronze statue of Dr. Martineau, by Miss Hope Pinker, daughter of the sculptor; in 1927, two Greek vases by Mrs. J. Estlin Carpenter; and in 1933 a framed painting of Dr. Martineau, by Mrs. Allingham, from Mr. Charles Wright.

Amongst recent donors of books may be mentioned Mrs. W. Haslam, Mrs. Albert Nicholson, Miss Sharpe, Revs. D. Walmsley B.A., C. J. Street M.A., L.L.B., Dendy Agate B.A., W. E. George M.A., H. W. Stephenson M.A., W. H. Drummond D.D., R. T. Herford D.D., Harold Rylett, W. L. Schroeder M.A., Messrs. Edgar Steinthal, James Groves, Exors of Dr. Lionel Tayler, Dr. C. G. Higginson, Hugo Talbot and the Misses Brooks. Dr. Higginson's gift (268 volumes) from the library of the late Rev. P. M. Higginson M.A., included a fine set of first editions of the works of his aunt, Miss Harriet Martineau.

With the death of the Rev. Alexander Gordon M.A., February 21, 1931, the Library came into possession of a large part of his valuable collection of books on Nonconformist history, including rare volumes purchased at home and abroad over a period of more than half a century, several valuable MSS. and his unique copy of the *Dictionary of National Biography* (sixty-nine volumes) presented by the Gaskell Scholarship Trustees. His executors then gave a collection of MS. letters and a number of rare prints and engravings.

Two of Gordon's oldest friends, both bachelors, quickly enriched the Library by their donations. The Rev. J. H. Bibby, an old student and donor since 1897 of the Greek prize, presented 660 volumes, including sets of the Home University Library and the Cambridge Manuals of Science and Literature, and the Rev. A. W. Fox M.A., who had served the College for long as Examiner and Visitor, added 1,000 volumes, mainly classical, biographical and literary in character, including many from the seventeenth and eighteenth centuries.

In October, 1933, Miss Philips, of The Park, Prestwich,

gave 120 volumes published in the seventeenth and eighteenth centuries from the library built up by her forbears, men prominent in the commercial, dissenting and political life of Manchester in the early part of last century; the Gaskell Scholarship Trustees made a grant covering the subscription to the *Dictionary of American Biography*; and the Unitarian Historical Society of America placed the Library on their free list, presenting a set of their publications from the beginning. Next month, on the dissolution of the Pioneer Preachers' Hostel, London, established in connection with the New Theology Movement led by the Rev. R. J. Campbell M.A., and since 1912 associated with Unitarians, 120 volumes were given to the Library.

In July, 1934, the Rev. J. Mason Bass M.A., Chairman of the Library Committee, gave 573 volumes, mostly modern, besides numerous reports and pamphlets. Subsequently, Mrs. A. B. Woodhouse, granddaughter of the first Principal, presented a case containing some 200 letters, following an earlier gift from Miss Mary Dendy M.A. of letters written by Harriet Martineau. Numerous letters and other documents were then given by Miss Harrison, which were written by various members of the Harrison family from the eighteenth century onwards.

By his will, the Rev. J. H. Bibby bequeathed in 1934 1,265 books, including a Shakespearian collection of 500 volumes, and many rare works on Irish Unitarian history. The manuscripts in the Library have increased steadily in number during the last decade, and in 1936 some 300 letters, written by or to Arian divines in the eighteenth century, were presented by Dr. A. J. Grieve, Principal of Lancashire Independent College.

In 1939 the Ministerial Fellowship, as the residuary legatee of the late Rev. Thomas Paxton, presented 250 volumes from his library, mainly biographical.

Recognition of the position which the Library had attained was shown by its inclusion (1927) by Dr. L. Newcombe in *The University and College Libraries of Great Britain and Ireland*; in *The Aslib Directory, A Guide to Sources of Specialised Information in Great Britain and Ireland* (1928); and, from 1930 in *Minerva Jahrbücher der gelehrten Welt*, a similar German publication; by the presentation to it (1933–1937) of a set of the *Letters of Sir Walter Scott*, given to all important libraries in the country by an anonymous admirer of Scott; and by the gift of the *Records of the Dutch Church, London*, from the sixteenth to the nineteenth century by the

Trustees of the Austin Friars Church, London. More recently, at the request of the Manchester City Librarian, the Library has been admitted as a constituent member of the North-West Regional Library System, and permission has been given to catalogue books in the College Library not included in the Free Reference Library in return for certain valuable concessions to students reading in the Library at Summerville.

The growth of the Library may be seen from the following figures, the only ones available: in 1857 the books were valued at £100; in 1873 they numbered 1,585; in 1876, 3,000; in 1882, 3,621; in 1911, 8,000; in 1917, 9,800; in 1923, 15,000; in 1936, 25,000; and in 1939, 27,000.

For some years, about a thousand volumes have been taken out every session by students and others, exclusive of those borrowed for use in the Library. The Library is open to *Alumni* of the College, ministers of the district, and university students provided with introductions.

II—Its Character

WORD of the collection as a whole. This is not, as its origin and use might suggest, altogether sombre and academic in character. Liberal dissenting ministers and laymen of an older generation, differing greatly from their evangelical contemporaries, did not eschew the literature of fiction, travel, or the stage. There is room for *Punch and Judy*, by George Cruikshank (1828) and *Pickwick* (with suppressed plates) (1836), whilst the great novelists of the nineteenth century, and some who hardly deserve the epithet " great "—the living alone almost wholly excepted—have their appointed place, a few in original editions. The exception does not mean that by the Nonconformist conscience a dead dog is esteemed more highly than a living lion, but only that fiction enters the Library by gift, not purchase, and that donors belonged to the now much despised Victorian age. Writers of fiction of the century before the last, though more " profane " in tone than their successors in the reign of Disraeli's patroness, are by no means wanting, e.g., *The Spiritual Quixote, or the Summer's Ramble of Mr. Geoffrey Wildgoose* (two volumes, 1774), written by Richard Graves, the clergyman poet-novelist, ridiculing Methodist enthusiasm and practice, is in the company of Rousseau's *La Nouvelle Heloise* (two editions, 1769, 1792), and Mary Wollstonecraft's *Original Stories from Real Life* (1790). English fiction occupies 470 volumes, and foreign fiction is not far behind. Travel and adventure, apart from reprints in Arber's *Garner,* are represented by names like Addison, Aikin, Boswell, Burnet, and Brooke in the eighteenth century, by those of Archer, Bird, Bryce, Burckhardt, Burton, Speke, Stanley, and Scott in the nineteenth century, and Nansen in the twentieth. The earliest is a folio by Herrera dated 1622. Amongst modern editions are Hakluyt in twelve volumes and Purchas in twenty. Of drama, not reckoning modern editions of the great English and foreign writers, there is a folio of the works of Davenant

c

(1673), another of Beaumont and Fletcher (1679), and two fine editions of these famous collaborators (ten volumes, 1750; four volumes, 1904–1912), together with a considerable number of plays from the eighteenth and early nineteenth centuries, exclusive of critical discussions of the drama, and a small collection of 500 volumes of Shakespeare and Shakespearian studies. On the other hand, amongst the fourteen works by William Prynne is the famous *Histrio-Mastix, The Players Scourge* (1635), a quarto of a thousand pages with a title-page of enormous length, a rare and valuable work, which led to his imprisonment and the loss of both ears.

English literature, especially poetry, is well represented, and there are comparatively few great writers from John Milton to Robert Browning of whom there is not at least one first edition —of Milton there are six. In addition to these, there are his *Collected Works,* ed. John Toland (three volumes, 1698), a 1708 edition of *Paradise Lost, Letters and Papers,* 1746, various modern editions of his prose and poetical works, and five standard lives of the Puritan Poet, including that of Masson in six volumes, besides several studies of his verse and doctrine. Minor poets and prose writers of the eighteenth century are very much in evidence.

To philosophy, as might be expected, a whole section of the Library is devoted, and amongst first editions are works of Bacon, Berkeley, Butler, Collins, Cudworth, Diderot, Hutcheson, Hartley, Law, Locke, Price, Priestley, Stewart, Hume, Fichte and Toplady—to name only writers of the seventeenth and eighteenth centuries. John Locke, as the great advocate of toleration and the founder of a philosophy and biblical criticism so long influential in Unitarian circles, is represented by eight first editions, two seconds, and collected works (three volumes, 1714; ten volumes, 1812), and several biographies, the first being that by Lord King (two volumes, 1830), whilst of Joseph Priestley there are no fewer than a hundred first editions of his writings, in addition to collected works, later re-publications, and many biographies.

Scripture being the court of appeal for eighteenth and early nineteenth century Unitarians, the literature on the Bible is extensive. Early editions of the text include a Hebrew Bible of 1580 and a Greek Testament of 1522, and the versions include Latin, Italian, French, Danish, Scots, Welsh, Erse, German, Modern Greek, and Magyar, with a large number in English from the seventeenth to the twentieth century.

Next to the Bible, biography with autobiography bulks largest, and its catholicity is remarkable. Dictionaries of biography number sixteen, and biographical collections over a hundred, in many more volumes. The latter begins with John Bale's work (second ed. Basel, 1557), said to be the first of such British works to appear in print, but containing almost every " Billingsgate phrase in the Latin language " in its abuse of Romanists. It begins a catalogue of British writers with " Samothes Gigas, who lived not long after the deluge," whilst Cave's *Scriptorum Ecclesiasticorum Historia Literaria* (1688) begins with Jesus Christ " on account of the celebrated epistle which he wrote to Abgarus "! Both works contain, of course, much that is in accessible elsewhere. Here, too, is Fuller's *Abel Redivivus,* a piece of hack-work, but the first biographical collection in English, as well as his more worthy *History of the Worthies* . . . of 1662, and Walton's *Lives.*

Of general history, no period, ancient, medieval, or modern, is unworthily represented, but it is the Stuart and Cromwellian period that is most adequately covered, since two most generous donors to the Library had a special interest in it. It is impossible to list even the seventeenth century folios and quartos— to say nothing of the tracts and sermons—which must always serve as primary sources for writers on the Stuarts and Cromwell. On the Protector there are twenty-five works in thirty-three volumes.

Diaries and letters claim a place of their own in the catalogue, whilst science and education are by no means excluded.

Hymnology, especially Unitarian, is prominent in the collection, and few indeed are the Unitarian Hymnals named in Julian's *Dictionary of Hymnology* absent from the Library.

Forty-two dictionaries in as many languages, from Ethiopic to Esperanto, and grammars of almost as many tongues may interest the student of philology, whilst of classics it must suffice to say that it would be difficult to name a writer not to be found in ancient or modern editions.

In Semitics there is a fair collection, including the standard grammars, dictionaries, inscriptions and texts in Arabic, Assyrian and Babylonian, Ethiopic, Syriac, Aramaic, and Hebrew; and for the seventeenth century, Buxtorf's *Lexicon* (1655), *Synagoga Judaica* (1604), *Tiberias* (1665), *Bythner's* works; Meyers' and Alexander's *Tephilloth* (1775), Midrash Rabba (1896), the works of Reland and Raschi. Of modern works, all Petermann's *Porta Linguorum Orientalium,* Field's *Hexapla,* Burkitt's *Evangelion Da-Mepharreshe,* etc. Three Hebrew grammars, additional to those mentioned elsewhere, deserve a brief note. *Lingua Eruditorum,* by Victor Bythner (1675), explaining the Hebrew alphabet, calls " resh " the " lingua canina, quod tremula linguae vibratione, canum, dum ringuntur, sonum imitatur," which may be rendered: " the canine letter, because (pronounced) with a tremulous vibration of the tongue, it is like the sound of dogs when they snarl." *The Key of the Holy Tongue* (Leyden, 1593) is by P. Martinus, " All Englished by John Udall for the benefit of those that (being ignorant of Latin) are desirous to know the Holy Tongue." Udall was a contributor to the Mar-Prelate Tracts and died, after imprisonment for his offence, the year before the grammar was published. This work, we are told, " was prized by James VI of Scotland, who enquired for the author on his arrival in England in 1603, and, on learning he was dead, exclaimed: " By my soul, then, the greatest scholar of Europe is dead." *The Elements of Hebrew Grammar* (1832), by William Probert (1790-1870), Minister of Walmsley Chapel, near Bolton, for nearly fifty years, has some special features of its own. Copies are extremely rare, and Professor T. Witton Davies, of Bangor, having long searched for it in vain, travelled to Manchester to get a glimpse of it. It was printed by private subscription, only a small edition was published, and this copy is due to a bequest from the family of one of the subscribers.

Eventually by the gift of a friend who desires to remain anonymous, the Library will come into possession of a collection of Hebrew and Jewish books numbering over 700 volumes. This collection includes *The Babylonian Talmud,* Wilna edition, 1880–1885, in twelve volumes; the modern English translation of the same, Soncino Press, in thirty-two volumes; *The Jerusalem Talmud,* in the editions of Krotoschin and Pietrokoff; *Mischnah, Tosephta, Mechilta, Siphra, Siphre, Tanchuma,* all in standard editions. There are many texts of works now out of print; Raymond Martini's *Pugio Fidei; Toledoth Jeshu,* in two editions; *Tela Ignea Satanae* (Wagenseil), and others. This collection, which is that of an expert in Talmudic studies, will enable the Library to take its place amongst the Hebrew libraries in the United Kingdom.

One rather uncommon feature of the Library is its relatively large proportion of books, of which copies have been publicly burnt. This is due to the comparative smallness of the collection and its inclusion of a large number of heretical books.

If, without consulting the catalogue of the Library, one desired to acquire some knowledge of its contents, it would be most helpful to read the essays of two celebrated men of letters, friends and Unitarians, whose lives covered the close of the eighteenth and the beginning of the nineteenth centuries.

William Hazlitt (1778–1836) was the son of a Unitarian divine, whose published works are in the Library, and was himself trained at Hackney College to follow his father's profession. His tribute to his father in *Dissenters and Dissenting Ministers* glows with the veneration of his person and love of his principles. His sketch of the favourite reading of the old ministers, obviously drawn from his memory of his father's library, describes books and authors at Summerville. "They had Neal's *History of the Puritans* by heart, and Calamy's *Account of the Two Thousand Ejected Ministers,* and gave it to their children to read—with the pictures of the polemical Baxter, the silver-tongued Bates, the mild-looking Calamy, and old honest Howe; they believed in Lardner's *Credibility of the Gospel History*; they were deep-read in the works of the Fratres Poloni, Pripscovius, Crellius, Cracovius—who sought out truth in the texts of Scripture and grew blind over Hebrew points." The last name in the list, apparently coined from that of the Polish city, probably indicates the writer's innocence of any personal acquaintance with the *Bibliotheca Fratrum Polonorum, quos Unitarios Vocant.* Doubtless the vellum backs of the folios and the pictures of their sad-looking authors were familiar, and such knowledge sufficed. It was otherwise with *John Buncle* (two volumes, 1765–1766), the work of Thomas Amory, a contributor, to Priestley's *Theological Repository.* In an essay on Buncle, he calls him "the English Rabelais," and his work "a Unitarian Romance." Besides those named, other authors noticed by Hazlitt, of whom early—in most cases first—editions are in the Library, are Burke, Fox, Tucker, Milton, Dryden, Pope, Thomson, Cowper, Swift, Rabelais, Voltaire, Gray, Goldsmith, Bacon, Sir Thomas Browne, Jeremy Taylor, Isaak Walton, Scott, Wordsworth, Leigh Hunt, Montaigne, Richardson, Sterne, Godwin, and Cobbett.

Similarly, Charles Lamb (1775–1834) names writers who may be read in the Library—Selden, Usher, Scapula, for whom George Dyer "might have mustered," Zimmerman on Solitude, Fulk Greville, Horne Tooke, Hume (and Smollett's Continuation of Hume), Sheridan, Locke. Dyer's works include the life of friend Robert Robinson (1796), described by Wordsworth as "one of the best biographies in the language," and this, with all Robinson's works, are in the Library.

Of the writers mentioned by Leigh Hunt, the friend of Hazlitt and Lamb, in his essay on *My Books*, all are here, with early editions of Petrarch (1525), Horace (1588), Spenser (1611), Dryden (1711), Pope (1729), and Prior (1717). *The Arabian Nights* is a modern edition (twelve volumes, 1897); the rest are eighteenth century editions, except Milton already named.

If to the books spoken of by Hazlitt, Lamb, and Hunt are added those quoted by Mark Pattison in his famous essay on the *Tendencis of Religious Thought in England 1688–1750*, and by Leslie Stephen in the *History of English Thought in the Eighteenth Century*, inspired by that essay, a formidable number of the inmates housed at Summerville would be identified, for there are only a few writers named who are absent from the collection, most of them, indeed, being here in their original editions, and Deism claiming 128 cards.

It must be confessed that, with conspicuous exceptions, these treatises of the seventeenth and eighteenth centuries are tedious reading—least tolerable of all, perhaps, the writings of Belsham and his school in their combative mood, for, as Hazlitt said, " It would be in vain to strew the flowers of poetry round the borders of the Unitarian controversy." The political orations of the preachers are a trifle less wearisome, but neither these nor the funeral sermons will keep one long out of bed. The latter, like the rest of their kind, are too lengthy and learned for our taste, and seldom descend to the particulars dear to the student of biography. When they do, and add bibliographies, as frequently happens, they are often invaluable, as affording all that is known of the deceased worthies. Dr. Albert Peel, writing on the contents of the New College Library, London, in the *Congregational Quarterly* (April, 1938) says: " A smile can always be raised by referring to this collection of funeral sermons, but only those who have engaged in historical research know what a mine of information they contain."

" How many of us have the desire, or for that matter the courage," asked Mr. Mark A. Thompson (*History*, December, 1935) " to read eighteenth century sermons? Macaulay was perhaps the last political historian of note to be conversant with these writings. Is it too much to hope that some brave spirit will make a study of them as sources for history, and impart his conclusions to the world?" When the " brave spirit " arrives, he might do worse than turn his attention to our Library. He will have need of the same industry as characterised not a few of the forgotten preachers.

A volume of *Funeral Sermons for Samuel Bourn,* of Bolton, who died March 4, 1719, in the seventy-second year of his age, includes one by his son of the same name preached to his father's late congregation. Even this is adorned with footnote quotations in Greek and Latin, and what the preacher said in praise of his departed sire may be applied with equal truth, if not in the same spirit of eulogy, to most other clerical authors of the age. "Nor need you to be told that *he sat down to work* for every sermon he preach'd; he did not put you off with jejune or trifling ministrations, with unfurnished discourses, they always smell'd of the lamp." The italics are the preacher's. Of many of the hundreds of sermons and pamphlets of the seventeenth and eighteenth centuries, the reader may be content to repeat the words of a scribe who wrote in one of them: "There appears to be much in this volume worth considering, even if some of his conclusions be rejected."

The great English sermons long since acknowledged as "literature" are here. Those belonging to the Elizabethan and later times named by Edmund Gosse in his article on "Sermons" (*Encyclopædia Britannica,* 11th ed.) are "the judicious Hooker," Henry Smith, "the prime preacher of the nation," Lancelot Andrewes, "the star of preachers," John Donne, Joseph Hall, John Hales, Edmund Calamy, Benjamin Whichcote, Richard Baxter, John Owen, Ralph Cudworth, Archbishop Leighton, Jeremy Taylor, Isaac Barrow, Robert Smith, John Tillotson, Edward Stillingfleet, Benjamin Hoadly, Joseph Butler, Thomas Boston, John Wesley, and George Whitfield. All are in the Library, mostly in original editions, save the last named, who is commended rather for his zeal as preacher than for the literary distinction of his discourses.

A leading article in *The Times Literary Supplement* (April 1, 1939) entitled "Our Debt to the Pulpit" mentions Thomas Adams, Jeremy Taylor, Thomas Chalmers, Joseph Butler, F. W. Robertson, and John Caird, all represented in the Library by first editions, and adds: "Contemporary with all of them have been hosts of preachers who have left no such memorials; and among that multitude unquestionably have been men of the greatest immediate power and influence. To their unrefined merits lettered arrogance must not deny praise; for with a rude preacher it is not as it is with an incondite poet; the great cloud of homely preachers, though standing outside literature, have also educated the nation when other educators there were none. . . . England has been the land of sermons as well as the Book, and its debt is almost as great to the one as it is to the other."

The nature and extent of that debt may be learnt, in no inconsiderable measure, from the collection at Summerville, whilst, in especial, the number of Unitarian sermons is probably not excelled in any English library.

The tracts in the Library, *mutatis mutandis,* resemble the sermons in range and variety. They include those of men famous wherever the English tongue is spoken and of others so obscure as to merely *vox et praeterea nihil.* An attempt has been made, not without success, to collect all those tracts and pamphlets which illustrate the thought and interests of the old Dissenters, and, particularly, of the several branches of Nonconformity represented in the General Assembly of Unitarian and Free Christian Churches. Such a collection is obviously not simply theological, and in itself may be said to express not only " the Nonconformist conscience " in politics and religion, but also indicate the extent to which Dissenters, from the date of their ejection from the Church, were sensitive to the claims and demands of life in a changing world. One difference between tracts and sermons is that in the former authors are not exclusively ministerial, a fact of no little significance for makers of chapel histories to whom pulpit personalities and their activities seem to be too commonly the alpha and omega of congregational life.

The classification of sermons and tracts in the catalogue indicates their character within the limits it provides. SERMONS: —American, American Memorial, American Ordination; British and Foreign Unitarian Association; Farewell; French; Memorial; Opening of Chapels; Ordination; Political; Provincial Assembly; Sixteenth Century; Seventeenth Century; Eighteenth Century; Nineteenth Century; Twentieth Century. TRACTS: —Agnostic; American; Anti-Clerical; Anti-Papal, Banking and Currency; Baptismal; Controversial; Controversy, Salters' Hall; Corn Laws; Dissent; Factory Acts; French; Hewley Case; Jewish Disabilities; Methodist; Political; Poor Laws; Scriptural; Trials; Unitarian; Sixteenth Century; Seventeenth Century; Eighteenth Century; Nineteenth Century; Twentieth Century.

Literature relating to all the Unitarian controversies of the three kingdoms during the last two centuries is here. The Salters' Hall Controversy (1719), " viewed by Unitarians as the charter of their liberties," has sixty-five cards to its credit, and the number of volumes illustrating *The Arian Movement in England* is so large that no fewer than seventy works mentioned by the Rev. J. H. Colligan in the book of that name published in Manchester in 1913 are in the collection, with others unnamed by him; though he apparently found many of them only in London and Edinburgh. Another Presbyterian historian speaks of one of our volumes, published in 1834, as " very rare," and went to Bristol to get a sight of it. Again, in the appendix to his Hartley Lecture on *The Revelation of John* (1919), Dr. A. S. Peake said: " So far as I know Evanson was the first to deny the unity of the Apocalypse. This was in *The Dissonance of the Four Generally Received Evangelists* (1792). The book is, I believe, scarce (I have seen no copy but my own). Schweitzer says: " Further information regarding this, as it seems, rather rare book would be desirable " *(Paul and His Interpreters)*. Two editions of the work named are in the Library together with the rest of the writings of its eccentric author, a Unitarian clergyman.

Students more interested in the movements of the twentieth than in those of the preceding two centuries will find in the Library materials for the history of three which aroused much controversy: —The New Theology Movement, The Free Catholic Movement, and the Liverpool Cathedral Discussion. The series of 130 periodicals, most of them complete or current, cover the Unitarian movement in the British Isles, and much else, whilst the collection of Unitarian Chapel histories is probably the most complete in the country.

The writings of Unitarians, by no means exclusively theological, many of which enjoyed but a limited circulation, are here, *e.g.* the Persian translations of Samuel Robinson. Samuel Robinson, of Wilmslow (1794–1884), a lay-student of Manchester College and later its president, published translations in verse of Horace, Dante, and Schiller, but his most notable translations were those of Persian poetry. His Oriental studies led him to correspond for ten years with Professor Wilhelm Bacher, of Buda Pesth. When the distinguished traveller and Orientalist, Arminius Vambéry, visited England in 1874, Robinson was asked to meet him at Stalybridge, and enquired if he knew Dr. Bacher. " My best pupil," Vambéry replied, and then remarked that he was specially charged by Dr. Bacher to find out " a ·Mr. Robinson," whom he intended to ask for at Oxford. He then learnt that " Mr. Robinson " was at his elbow.

Sir John Bowring, President of the College in 1870, another translator of foreign literature, has a dozen volumes in the Library. He was Jeremy Bentham's executor, and a rare volume of the latter had been loaned by the Library to the late Professor C. E. Vaughan, formerly Professor of English Literature at Leeds, when he died.

Lest it should be imagined that the Library has no interest for good churchmen, it should be said that the collection of liturgies is not to be despised, early fathers are well to the fore in folio, quarto, and octavo; that there are *Lives of the Saints,* by S. Baring Gould (sixteen volumes), *Lives of the English Saints,* edited by J. H. Newman (six volumes), *Lives of the Irish Saints,* by J. O'Hanlon (ten volumes), Hook's *Ecclesiastical Biography* (eight volumes, 1845–1852), *Tracts for the Times* (six volumes), half a dozen lives of Newman, twenty-five volumes from his pen, with several editions of the *Apologia,* including the original one of the pamphlets as they fell from the press in 1864, besides many histories of the Church dating from the seventeenth to the twentieth century. The great English churchmen have their place. Of Richard Hooker, perhaps the greatest of them all, there is the folio edited by Gauden (1662) and the standard modern edition by Church and Paget (three volumes, 1888) together with Paget's *Introduction to the Fifth Book of the Ecclesiastical Polity* (1899) and a nineteenth century edition in two volumes by Dobson, besides sermons from the seventeenth century and a *Digest of the Polity* (1840).

Similarly, Methodism, the great but despised daughter of the established Church, may be studied here in some of the classical writings of her sons: —Wesley's Journal (five volumes, 1797), together with that of Curnock (eight volumes, 1910–1916), his *Letters,* edited by Priestley (1791), and by Telford (eight volumes, 1931); his life by Hampton (three volumes, 1791), Southey (two volumes, 1820), Moore (two volumes, 1824), and several lives and studies of this century and the last; a few early writings of Wesley himself and his collected *Works* (fourteen volumes, 1856), the lives of his greatest co-adjutors, modern histories of Methodism, and of her progeny now happily returned to Mother Church; the *Lives of Early Methodist Preachers,* edited by Thomas Jackson (six volumes, 1873), and a small collection of tracts relating to the birthpangs of Methodist offspring. In particular, movements originated by Joseph Cooke (1775–1811) and Joseph Barker (1806–1878), which ultimately added to the strength of Unitarianism in the northern counties, are very completely represented by tracts, sermons, biographies, and periodicals.

Doubtless Methodism may be seen at her best in one of her own college libraries, but it cannot be said that she makes a poor show on the shelves of the Unitarian College Library.

Naturally, with their longer pedigrees and more intimate association with the Unitarian Movement, Presbyterians, Congregationals, Baptists, and Quakers occupy a larger place in the Library, alike in biography, history, theology, and controversy. Indeed, in Nonconformist, and particularly in Unitarian history, the Library possesses one of the finest collections in the North of England, and not a few volumes absent from the great English libraries. With a single exception, every book mentioned by Principal Odgers in 1882 as wanting is now here, with very many others unnamed by him, whilst the collection of the old *Unitarian Tracts* is almost certainly more complete than any other. Moreover, a number of tracts by John Wallis (1616–1702), bound up with one volume of the *Unitarian Tracts*, were formerly in the possession of Stephen Nye (1648–1719), the chief Unitarian clergyman responsible for the Unitarian publications, and contains manuscript notes by him, and a volume on *The Seventeenth Century Unitarian Tracts*, an expansion by typescript additions of an essay published in 1923, presents the most complete discussion of these writings, mostly anonymous, available in any library.

A copy of *Irenicum Irenicorum* (1658), an antitrinitarian writing published anonymously by Daniel Zwicker, gave rise to much controversy in the seventeenth century. According to Alexander Gordon (*Journal of the Friends Historical Society,* October, 1912) a copy of it was presented by John Knowles, the first English Arian preacher, to Henry Hedworth, a Cromwellian captain to whom the first of the Unitarian tracts was dedicated by Stephen Nye. Gordon's copy in the Library, purchased at Stuttgart, June, 1912, was obtained, in his own words, " after twenty years' search, and at the cost of more shillings than its weight or worth."

As both sides of most controversies are represented, it follows that occasionally the works of bitter foes, like Wallis and Nye, rest peaceably side by side on the same shelf. So is it with the Deists and their opponents in the eighteenth century, and a volume of sermons preached before the Long Parliament by various divines in 1642 has a companion volume of discourses (1660) delivered before King Charles II on his return from his travels.

Books " privately printed " or " printed for private circulation," and therefore scarce, are numerous. Amongst them are
the Journals of his Travels, by Robert Heywood (1768–1868).
He was the second Mayor of Bolton, a lifelong member of
Bank Street Chapel, which he served in various capacities, and
a life member of the British Association. He was a guardian
of the poor, a borough and a county magistrate, and for
fifty-two years secretary of the Bolton Infirmary and Dispen-
sary. From 1837 to 1868 he was treasurer of the Widows'
Fund Association (established 1764). For a Lancastrian of that
period, he travelled widely—to Italy, 1826, America, 1834, The
Levant, 1845, and Russia, 1858. The journals remained in
manuscript from sixty-one to ninety-three years before being
published, 100 copies only, four volumes, in 1919. They are
of considerable interest to students alike of the economics,
politics, and religion of the second quarter of the nineteenth
century.

A small collection of works by Mystics, especially Boehme,
and another of Muggletonians—all from the seventeenth and
eighteenth centuries—add unexpected variety to the Library,
and several volumes on the " occult " include two quartos from
the sixteenth century, together with a few works on astrology,
including Lilly's masterpiece of 1647.

Mr. Holbrook, in his *Anatomy of Bibliomania*, has no chapter
on " Quaint Titles," otherwise he might have included in one
section of it a few of those at Summerville, *e.g. Dialogues of
the Dead, Letters from Hell, The Autobiography of Satan,
The Political History of the Devil, The Autobiography of Jesus
of Nazareth, The Diary of Judas Iscariot,* and, possibly,
Eutychus and His Relations.

Lamb, in " Detached Thoughts on Books and Reading,"
speaks of " books which are no books—' biblia a-biblia.' " All
the authors to whom, rightly or wrongly, he attributes such
productions are here—Hume, Gibbon, Robertson, Beattie,
Soame Jenyns, Josephus, and Paley—and, as substitutes for
his " court calendars, directories, pocket books, draught boards
bound and lettered at the back, almanacks, and statutes at
large," we have university calendars, proceedings, annual reports,
cabinets of newspaper cuttings and photographs, albums, and
catalogues.

The last named, however, are not without their attractions
for book-lovers. Upwards of fifty in number, they include,

besides modern publications, many of other libraries, the earliest being that of the Chetham Library (three volumes, 1791, 1826); also *Books Written by Friends* (three volumes, 1867, 1893); *The Term Catalogues, 1668-1709*, edited by Edward Arber (three volumes, 1903-1906), being No. 69 of a quarto edition of 100 signed by the editor; *Bibliographia Boltoniensis*, No. 169 of an edition of 300 (1913); *A Baptist Bibliography* (two volumes, 1916, 1922), and the catalogues of a number of scholars from 1816 on with the prices of books marked.

The *Catalogus Bibliotheca Harleianæ* (three volumes, 1743) contains an "account of the Harleian Library" written by no less a person than Samuel Johnson. The words "apud Thomam Osborne" at the foot of the title-page bring to mind the publisher for whom the great lexicographer slaved in the days of his penury. "It was said," reports Boswell, "that Johnson one day knocked Osborne down in his shop, with a folio, and put his foot upon his neck. The simple truth I had from Johnson himself: 'Sir, he was impertinent to me, and I beat him, but it was not in his shop, it was in my own chamber.'" Leslie Stephen identified the book in a Septuagint folio of 1594, and said it was in existence in a bookseller's shop at Cambridge in 1812.

Amongst other "biblia-a-biblia" in the Library may be included many volumes of lectures and notes of lectures in manuscript, and manuscript sermons elsewhere discussed. To these may be added a stout quarto volume labelled *Test Act Papers*, collected by William Wood (1745-1808), which is made up of fly-sheets, proceedings of deputies all over the country, and letters to and from politicians like William Wilberforce, Henry Duncombe, Henry Beaufoy, Christopher Wyvill, and Lord Petrie relating to the movement of Dissenters to obtain relief from the iniquitous legislation of the High-Church Party. William Wood, then Minister of Mill Hill Chapel, Leeds, was the leading spirit in the West Riding campaign on this question. Another volume deserving to come under Lamb's curious classification is one in MS. labelled *Select Hymns*, dated 1766. Its author, John Crossley, whose pedigree is like that of Melchizidek, has signed his name thrice in different cryptic forms, and at the end of the book written tables of passages from the two Testaments supposed to illustrate doctrines in which he was interested. A third volume which has claims to be included amongst "biblia-a-biblia" is entitled *The Sozzini and Their School*, by Alexander Gordon. It is made up of two remarkable articles contributed in 1879 to *The Theological*

Review, expanded and revised in manuscript by their author in preparation for a volume which was announced by Messrs. Putnam in 1911 under the title of "Laelius and Faustus Socinus" in the series of *Heroes of the Reformation,* but unfortunately never published. The numerous notes and corrections in Gordon's interleaved copy of the articles have been typed and inserted in the text of the bound volume, wherein may be found the results of more than thiry years' research by one who wrote on the Sozzini in the ninth and the eleventh editions of the *Encyclopædia Britannica.*

Two other volumes similarly extended are *Education under the Test Acts, Being the History of the Nonconformist Academies,* and a *Biography of Alexander Gordon,* to both of which considerable additions have been made in typescript, including in the latter an index to the valuable reviews of biographical and historical books, contributed for many years to *The Christian Life,* which are invaluable to the student of Nonconformist history.

One example of a "grangerised" volume is *Original Letters and Papers addressed to Oliver Cromwell,* found among the papers of John Milton, edited by John Nickolls, 1743, in which are inserted a biographical account of Cromwell, four portraits of him and one of Milton; another is *Views in North Britain Illustrative of the Works of Robert Burns . . .* by James Storer and John Greig, which contains numerous additional illustrations together with excerpts from printed sources relating to the poet. Granger himself is here, *A Biographical History of England,* five volumes, 1769–1774, with the three supplementary volumes by Noble, 1806.

Of "bowdlerised" works, there is the father of them all, the once popular *Family Shakespeare* in ten volumes "in which nothing is added to the original text; but those words are omitted which cannot with propriety be read aloud in a family." It ran to seven editions. This is the fourth, published in 1825.

A curious and unique volume in the Library is *The Manchester Socinian Controversy,* published anonymously in 1825. It is interleaved and contains manuscript notes, biographical and historical, excerpts from original authorities, copies of letters from the seventeenth century on, identifications of contributors and of persons mentioned in the text, together with five added illustrations, of which four were made in colour for this book. The notes were made by the owner of the book,

George Hadfield (1799–1879), one of the principals in the controversy and in the Lady Hewley litigation which followed. He was a "malleus Unitariorum," and is said to have chosen his pew in Cross Street Chapel, Manchester, when the Unitarians should have been dispossessed of all their places of worship by the Independents as the result of the verdict in the Hewley suit. His signature is given several times, and the dates of every entry in the book from 1825 to 1871. The volume forms the most complete evidence available for the controversy to which it relates, and is indispensable for the study of the legal suit already named, full records of which are also in the Library.

Though Dissent is the prevailing "note" of the Library, which, at least indirectly, is largely the creation of men excluded from the ancient seats of learning, the two great English universities are reflected in all their glory, not only by many folios and quartos from their presses, but also, amongst other books, by Antony Wood's *Historia et Antiquitates Universitatis Oxoniensis* (folio, 1674), his *Athenæ Oxonienses,* edited by P. Bliss (four volumes, 1813–1820), and Fuller's *History of the University of Cambridge* (folio, 1655) with *Athenæ Cantabrigienses,* by C. H. and T. Cooper (two volumes, 1858–1861). Moreover, Aubrey's *Lives,* so closely connected with Antony Wood's works and with Oxford (two volumes, 1813), and the modern edition edited by A. Clark (two volumes, 1898) are both here.

Amongst early books may be mentioned two which give what has long been esteemed the foundation of English political liberty, of which Unitarians early and late have been amongst the most stalwart defenders, viz. *Magna Carta Cum Aliis Antiquis Statutis,* published by Thomas Berthelet, 1540, and a translation of these documents by George Ferrers, 1541, " out of latyn or frenshe Imprinted at London in fletestreete by Elizabeth Wydow of Robert Redma dwellyng at the sygne of the George next to saynte Dunstones churche." Magna Carta was first printed in 1499, but not from the original text until 1759.

Authors include men and women of every class from king to peasant, the royal penmen being James I and Charles I. *The Workes of the Most High and Mighty Prince James* (folio, 1616) formerly rested in the library of the " Champion Dymoke," and contains his bookplate. It was the duty of the King's Champion at the beginning of the coronation banquet formally to challenge to combat any person who disputed the sovereign's title to the throne. The first Champion died in 1381. Sir Edward Dymoke (d.1625) was Champion at the coronation of James I, and the last occasion on which the Champion appeared was at the coronation of George IV, July 19, 1821.

The Workes of that Great Monarch and Glorious Martyr King Charles (1646) includes besides letters, speeches, etc., the *Eikon Basilike,* probably written by Bishop Gauden.

" Libraries," said Drummond of Hawthornden, " are as forests in which not only tall cedars and oaks are to be found, but bushes too, and dwarfish shrubs." It remains to add, as a matter of curious interest, that the largest volume in the Library is Foxe's *Actes and Monuments* (folio, 1596), weighing 18 lb. 10 oz., and the smallest, weighing $2\frac{1}{4}$ oz., is one of Pickering's Classics (1824), though this is separated by less than a quarter of an ounce from a Plantin Classic of 1634. The difference in the size of books as this relates to authors is characteristically set forth by Thomas Fuller in *The Appeal of Injured Innocence,* in reply to his contemporary, Peter Heylyn. " It is the advantage of a small book that the author's eye may in a manner be incumbent at once over it all, from the beginning to the end thereof; a cause why they may be more exactly corrected. A garden hard by one's house is easier weeded and trimmed than a field lying at some distance. Books which swell to a great volume cannot be spun with so even a thread, but will run coarser here and there; yea, and have knots in them sometimes, whereof the author is not so sensible as the reader; as the faults in children are not so soon found in them by their own fathers, as by strangers." Both the controversialists named are very well represented in the Library.

In its way the Library is a collection of bookplates from the seventeenth century on, a few of which are mentioned in what follows. One is of peculiar interest, namely that of the Rev. J. H. Bibby, who bequeathed his books to the Library. It is the work of John Vinycomb (1832–1928), one of the leading figures in this branch of art in the nineteenth century. It is printed in his volume on *The Production of Ex-Libris,* 1894. A pen and ink drawing reproduced by photo-lithography of a library interior, it has two B's (for Bibby) in the left-hand corner, an owl (for wisdom) in the right, and a bearded scholar in cap and gown reading at a table with his left hand on an hour glass. The declining sun is seen, and beneath the table is a globe and a death's head turned towards the scholar.

The four inscriptions are: "Live Simply, Think Highly, Work Truly, Serve Loyally." Under the picture, between two bees flying in opposite directions, is the subscription: "hys Boke. 'Tis mine and it is likewise yours, but an if this will not do, let it be mine goode friend, for I am the poorer of the two."

Vinycomb was a member of the Non-Subscribing Presbyterian Church of Ireland of which Bibby, an *alumnus* of the College, was for fifty-one years a minister. Vinycomb was also a lifelong friend of Hugh Thomson, the artist, upon whom in early days he exercised a great influence. In *Hugh Thomson, His Art, His Letters, His Humour and His Charm,* by M. H. Spielmann and Walter Jerrold (1931) there is a portrait of Vinycomb, who is described as Thomson's "well-loved instructor and mentor." An extract from a letter of the artist to Vinycomb acknowledges his "fine work as a designer, illuminator, and heraldic painter" in response to a preface to the catalogue of the Ulster Arts Exhibition (1906) in which Vinycomb had told something of Thomson's early life. Both the books named above were among the Bibby collection bequeathed to the College, and contain his bookplate.

The Unitarian College Library may fairly be described as a good, if not very extensive, collection, of peculiar interest to Nonconformists, but not without its appeal to the general reader; rich in works of reference, especially biographical, and, in its range and intrinsic value, having regard to its origin and history, a Library of which Unitarians have every reason to be proud.

D

III—Bibliography

T would be too much to claim that the Library has much of peculiar interest to bibliographers. There are no incunabula, or books printed in the fifteenth century, but most of the famous presses of the sixteenth century are well represented, e.g. Aldus, Venice; Gryphius, Lyons; Stephanus, Paris; and Froben, Basel; whilst the seventeenth and eighteenth century presses are very numerous, including Elzevir and Plantin from the one, and Foulis and Baskerville from the other.

The rare Servetus volumes are: (1) a copy of the first edition of Servetus' *De Trinitatis Erroribus* (16mo, 1531); (2) a copy of the first edition of *Dialogorum De Trinitate Libri Duo* (16mo, 1532); both the above are in unique conditions, in strictly contemporaneous binding, and bound with them are two other contemporary tracts—one against Erasmus; (3) a copy of the Venice edition of Servetus' *De Syrupis* (1545), revised by himself from the first Paris edition. Mr. Leonard Mackail, who has made a close study of the bibliography of Servetus, says:[1] " The genuine original editions of the 1531 and 1532 volumes on the Trinity (printed by Johann Setzer in Hagenau, near Strasburg) have for centuries been so extremely rare that it is not surprising that Osler, Cuthbertson, and Hemmeter give an illustration of a counterfeit instead." In a letter to the writer he identified the copy at Summerville as the Morante-Knaake copy, and gave particulars of its appearance at sales on the Continent in 1839, 1859, 1872, and 1907. In a Vienna catalogue, 1935, the first-named tract was priced at £84 and the statement made that at a Swiss auction in 1934 a copy fetched £126. For an eighteenth century reprint of the second tract £25 was asked.

Amongst the MS. notes in the Dutch translation of Servetus' *De Trinitate Erroribus,* by R(enier) T(elle), 1620, is a quotation from Henry, *Calvin, His Life and Times:* " The printer of this book was put to death." Another note on the title-page written

---

[1] Contributions to *Medical and Biological Research,* dedicated to Sir William Osler (1919), p. 769.

in Latin calls attention to the singular fact, discussed recently by Dr. Earl Morse Wilbur,[1] that "the translation of the *Dialogues* promised on the title-page and in the table of contents was omitted." The volume was not published until six years after Telle's death, owing to the warning of Episcopius "of the evils that might result from publication." The copy of Allwoerden's *Historia Michaelis Serveti* (1728), previously owned by Dr. Samuel Parr (1747–1825) and John Jebb, Bishop of Limerick (1775–1833), contains two long MS. notes, one of which is an extract from a letter of Desmaiseux in the *Bibliothèque raisonnée des ouvrages de l'Europe*. This makes plain that Servetus borrowed his comments on Moses in his edition of Ptolemy from Pirckheimer, who published his work in 1525, and so was not open to the charge which formed one of the counts in Calvin's indictment leading to his death. This edition of the book is the original—two editions in Latin being published. Another book, the outcome of the burning of Servetus by Calvin, *Contra Libellum Calvini*, is attributed to Castellio by Calvin, to Laelius Socinus by Sandius, and by Bock to neither. A French note on the fly-sheet describes it as a "Livre de la plus grande rareté." Ferdinand Buisson has settled the question of authorship in favour of Castellio,[2] but its date, or rather the interpretation of the Roman figures at the foot of the title-page, presents a problem not yet solved. Originally printed in 1554, of which edition no copy appears to have survived, it was reprinted in Holland "Anno Domini MDI.C X I I. Some scholars have read this as 1562, others as 1612, and a few as 1662. Buisson quotes a conjecture of Henri Bordier that the editors wished to put the two dates together under this singular form, the third numeral read as L, making it 1562, but if regarded as a typographical error making it 1612—the real date.[3] Wallace declares, and our copy suggests he is right, that it is not L but I with a point, so printed as to give it that appearance. "But," he adds, "there seems to be little reason to doubt that it is a typographical error, the printer having, through mistake, substituted the type of an I followed by a period, for one of the spaces sometimes used by printers, to display the letters on a title-page."[4] The Library copy has MS. notes referring to Wallace and other writers on the subject, and a note by Alexander Gordon to the effect

---

[1] Harvard Theological Studies XVII. *The two Treatises of Servetus on the Trinity* (1932), p. VIII.

[2] *Sebastien Castello.* T. 2, p. 365.

[3] Ibid.

[4] *Anti-Trinitarian Biography*, II, p. 90.

that the book belonged to the Rev. Edward Tagart, and that a copy in the British Museum has a later title-page (quoted *in extenso*) with no place or date of publication.

In *A Tragedy of the Reformation, Being the Authentic Narrative of the History and Burning of the " Christianismi Restitutio, 1553,* by David Cuthbertson (1912), there are many corrections, and a note signed " A.G.: Hardly a page in this book without a blunder." A copy of *Christianismi Restitutio* was burned with Servetus, and only three copies are now known, the one at Edinburgh, another at Paris, and the third at Vienna.

Of a contemporary of Servetus, the Italian Giacomo Contio, better known as Acontius, the sixteenth century philosopher and theologian, whose birth and death dates are uncertain, the Library possesses four copies of his *Stratagemata Satanæ,* first published at Basel in 1565; viz. the first English edition, Oxford, 1631, the Amsterdam edition, 1652, the anonymous English translation (which contains only four of the eight books), London, 1648, and the modern critical edition, edited by G. Koehler, 1927. The Amsterdam copy, purchased by John Kentish in 1816, contains a bibliographical note. " Acontius was excommunicated by Grindal, Bishop of London, for denying that Christ's taking flesh of the Virgin was a fundamental article of faith, and the English translation (by John Goodwin, the republican Independent) was prohibited by the Westminster Assembly and its author condemned as a heretic." The life of Acontius, written by H. R. Tedder, is in the *D.N.B.,* and in the copy formerly owned by Alexander Gordon there are several important corrections of the text, *e.g.* " The Apostles' Creed contains all necessary doctrine." " This is precisely contrary to Contio's view; in both the 1565 edns. of the Stratagemata (which differ not only in type but in content) he discusses the point (there are two different discussions), and decides against the adequacy of the App. Creed." Again, " His Arianism can scarcely be doubted." " This is nonsense; there is no trace of this particular heresy in his writings; he was thought to favour the Mennonite *i.e.* Valentinian view of Christ, simply because he pleaded that it was not a fundamental error." " As regards his birth; I think that if the writer had looked at Ch. Waddington ' Dict. des Sci. Philos,' or Bonet-Maury's ' Early Sources of Unitarian Christianity ' (translation), he would have thought 1520 nearer than 1500. As regards his death; June 6, 1566, given to his letter by Crenius is certainly a misprint or mistranscription, for this letter is incorporated into the Stratagemata bk. III, 1565. Grasser is no doubt right in

saying that he died shortly after the issue of the Stratagemata."
A later note by Alexander Gordon runs " Copy (of 1565 ed.)
in B.M., acquired 1893."

One of our first editions of Calvin, *Commentarius in Isaiam
Prophetam*, 1551, was formerly in the library of Archbishop
Trench (1807–1886), and contains the autographs of Adam
Bothwell, Bishop of Orkney (d. 1593), of David Forrest, reader
at Darsluke, 1574–1596, and of Archbishop Hamilton, of
Cashel, 1630.

Dialogi IV, by Castellio, printed at Goude, 1623, as
Alexander Gordon notes in it, contains " Prefixed the first prose
publication by F. P. Sozzini." Two of our three volumes by
Bernardino Ochino (1477–1564) were translated by Castellio,
and are very scarce. *De Purgatorio dialogue* was published
"apud Gesneros " at Tiguri (Zurich), 1556. The translator's
preface is dated December 6, 1555. It was translated by
Dr. Thaddaeus Dunus. *Liber De Corporis Christi Praesentia
in Coenae Sacramento* was published at Basel, 1561, and translated by Castellio, as was *Dialogue II*, Basel, 1563. The
dialogues led to Ochino's banishment from Zurich. The book
formerly belonged to Dr. J. R. Beard.

Two volumes by Francis David, the first Unitarian bishop
in Hungary, published at Kolozsvár, Transylvania, in 1571, are
memorials of the beginning of the oldest Unitarian movement,
with which the College is connected by means of the Sharpe
Hungarian Scholarship (est. 1911), which regularly brings
students to Manchester from Kolozsvár. One inscribed "liber
rarissimus," by John James Tayler, had been presented to him
at Budapest by Alexis Jacab, the biographer of Francis David.
To David we owe the first Edict of Toleration in Europe,
that of Torda in 1568, which gave protection to Roman
Catholics, Lutherans, Calvinists, and Unitarians, and has never
been revoked. The Hungarian Unitarian Church claims to be
the only one in Europe which, from its foundation, has enjoyed
legal protection. That it suffered persecution, however, is
shown by the history of another volume in the Library.
Enyedino's *Explicationes Locorum Veteris et Novi Testamenti*
. . . was presented to John Fretwell by the Consistory of the
Hungarian Church in recognition of his labours in its behalf.
It is said by John Kenrick to be " an enlargement of an unpublished treatise by Stephen Basilu, formerly minister of the
Saxon Church in Kolozsvár." This is the original edition published posthumously without date or place in 1598 or 1599. It
was publicly burnt in Transylvania and interdicted throughout

the German Empire. It is accordingly very rare. The second edition, in Hungarian, was published in 1619 at Kolozsvár, and the third edition in the following year. A fourth edition, with neither date nor imprint, was published at Groningen in 1670. The late Bishop Ferencz said that a copy of this book is in the Vatican Library catalogued as *Diabolus Invictissimus.*

Several volumes printed at Rakow serve to remind members of a free university faculty of theology in Manchester of a Polish Unitarian College, open to all comers in the early part of the seventeenth century, which was completely destroyed through the machinations of Jesuits. The Socinian Press had been founded by Alexius Radecki at Cracow, where the works of Socinus were first published during the reign of Stephen Bathory (1576–1586), and when suppressed in Cracow the press was transferred to Raków. Radecki was twice imprisoned for publishing Socinian literature, and for safety frequently printed under an assumed name. He was succeeded at Raków by his son-in-law, Sebastian Sternacki, by whom most of the volumes here were published. In one tract, by Jonas Schlichting, 1651, there is a reference to the press and its final suppression. Four from Raków dated 1618 are by Faustus Socinus, one of which, *Concionis Christi,* was formerly in the library of John Geisteranus, a Dutch antitrinitarian; a fifth, 1636, is by Peter Morscovius from lectures by John Crell; and a sixth, *De Uno Deo Patre,* 1631, is by John Crell.

The last named was read by a German, who wrote on the title-page his detestation of its doctrine. An English scribe on the opposite page says: " This edition is considerably enlarged and has escaped the attention of Bock." Two copies of the anonymous translation of Crell's book, entitled *The Two Books of John Crellius Francus, Touching One God the Father,* were " printed in Kosmoburg, at the sign of the Sun-beames in the Year of our Lord M.D.C.L.X.V." "Kosmoburg" is London. The publisher was Richard Moore at the Seven Stars in St. Paul's Churchyard. During the Commonwealth he published under his own name. On the restoration of Charles II this became unsafe. One of the copies has the title-page in black, the other in red, otherwise they are identical. In the former a long note in French gives a brief and unsympathetic account of the author. John Crell was a German scholar, Professor, 1613–1616, and Rector, 1616–1621, of the Socinian College at Rakow, and his works were included in the *Bibliotheca Fratrum Polonorum quos Unitarios vocant.*

Bock, named above, published the *Historia Antitrinitariorum* (two volumes) in 1784. It is based largely upon the *Bibliotheca Anti-Trinitariorium*, by Sandius, 1684, which gives only one edition of Crell in 1631, but three others in later years. In one of two copies of Sandius is a note signed " Edward Harwood." " This is a scarce and a very valuable book. It contains a very exact catalogue of the Arian and Unitarian writers and their writings. Its worth was announced to me by a learned foreigner. Sandius was a physician. He died at Amsterdam in 1680."

Two volumes by Adam Goslavius, printed at Rakow by Sternacki, 1613, 1620, are exceedingly rare—the second so much so that, as a Latin note on the title-page says: " Lubienicius, *History of the Polish Reformation,* was of opinion that this " incuria " of his friend had perished, and Feltnerus, *History of Crypto-Socinianism,* doubted its existence." Sandius, however, mentions both. Of the *Apologia Fratrum Unitariorum,* by F. Horvath, a Hungarian librarian has said in an inserted note: " This work was supposed for long to be extant only in the single copy in the Unitarian School at Szekely Keresztur." Our copy lacks title-page.

There are three copies of the Racovian Catechism in Latin; one, 18mo, pp. 279, printed at Rákow, M.D.C.I.X., another, extending to 317 pages on smaller paper, printed there in 1609. Thomas Rees, who translated the Catechism into English in 1818, thinks the former " is the original, and that the latter was printed subsequently in Holland." The first copy, in addition to a bibliographical note by Alexander Gordon, contains a remark by a former owner: " The original edition printed at Rákow, Very scarce." The second copy contains two notes: " Has the errata counted, which are noted in edition M.D.C.L.X.," and a later note by Gordon: " Dutch reprint in 1614." The third copy (1652) has also two notes; one by the Rev. William Bruce (1790–1868): " Printed in London. All copies ordered to be seized and burnt by Parliament 2 Ap. 1652." Gordon's note runs: " The Thomason copy (in the British Museum) with this same title-page has ' Catechesis ' only, dates it ' March,' and writes ' Londini ' over ' Racoviae ' crossed out. A.G. 26 Jany, 1917." In a subsequent article in the *Transactions of the Unitarian Historical Society* (1928), he quotes Thomas Rees: " This edition is exceedingly rare. It is mentioned in no foreign work relating to the Racovian Catechism, and the only copy I have seen is in the British Museum." Gordon adds: " There are two copies of this rarity at the Museum; there is also one at the Unitarian College in Manchester." He then proceeds to prove the date (March) given by the Thomason copy to be correct, showing that "the notice of Parliament was attracted to it with little or no delay."

There is more to be said. According to a minute of the Council dated "Tuesday, Jan. 21 (1651/2), as we learn from Masson (Life of Milton IV. 423), it was resolved 'That a warrant be issued to the Sergeant of Arms to repair to the house of William Dugard, printer, and there to make seizure of a certain impression of books entitled *Catechesis Ecclesiarum Poloniae,* and to require him to come forthwith to the Council.'" Masson adds: "Whether from sympathy with its views, or merely in the interests of literary curiosity and free discussion, Dugard, the Council of State's own printer, had passed an English edition of it through his press; and for this he was now in trouble." A little later he notes the proceedings of the House: "Mr. Millington reported "That Mr. William Dugard is the printer of the Book" his examination and that of others, and, finally, "and the Examination of Mr. John Milton, and a Note under the hand of Mr. John Milton of the 10th of August, 1650." "What may have been the nature of Milton's concern in the affair," Masson says, "we do not know. Was the note under his hand, of August 10, 1650, anything to which Dugard could refer as a permission or recommendation to print the book, received from the Council of State's own Latin Secretary at the very beginning of Dugard's printing-connexion with the Council?" Then, in a footnote he corrects his former opinion of the book. "I infer that Dugard's edition had been in Latin, and that the notoriety it had obtained had led to the more daring act of a publication of the same in English. There are extant copies of an English Translation of the Catechism, dated 1652; but it purports to have been printed at Amsterdam."

If Milton's "note" had survived, it might have thrown some light on his Anti-Trinitarianism. He was certainly responsible for what was printed by Dugard at this date, and it is known that before 1650 he was seriously engaged in investigating for himself the doctrine of the Scriptures in the original tongues, and was famous for his advocacy of freedom of the Press and full toleration of what were then known as the "sectaries."

There are in the Library two copies of the English translation of the Catechism, said to be "Printed at Amsterledam for Brooer Janz 1652." One is bound up with tracts written by John Bidle, and Joshua Toulmin conjectured that the translation was by him. "Amsterledam" is a mere subterfuge, and

Gordon thought " Brooer Janz " is Bidle. The English translation omits the original dedication to James I, has a preface of its own, and takes liberties with the text.

Edward Harwood (1720–1794), whose note on Sandius has been given, was the author of numerous works. In fact he claimed to have "written more books than any person now living except Joseph Priestley." Many are in the Library, including his edition of the Greek Testament, 1776, and *A Liberal Translation of the New Testament,* 1768. The latter a rare book, is an unhappy "attempt to translate the sacred writers with the same freedom, spirit, and elegance with which other English translations from the Greek classics have lately been executed." The result is that the familiar Parable of the Prodigal Son begins thus: " A gentleman of a splendid family and opulent fortune had two sons. One day the younger approached his father, and begged him in the most importune and soothing terms to make a partition of his effects between himself and his elder brother. The indulgent father, overcome by his blandishments, immediately divided all his fortunes between them." The former, in two volumes, includes *A View of the Principal Editions of the Greek Testament and of the Principal Critics of it.* It was a work as original in plan as it was admirable in execution. Harwood was the first to set aside altogether the traditional " received " text, and build up, direct from manuscript authorities, the text of his edition. Though passed over in silence by Scrivener and Sir Frederick Kenyon, it has been recognised as a pioneer work of great merit by Reuss, Abbot, Gregory, and Dr. Souter. The same is true of the anonymous text and version by Daniel Mace (1720), a Presbyterian minister of Arian opinion, wrongly identified by Scrivener, Gregory, and Abbot as " William Mace, a Gresham lecturer " who died in 1767. This work, copies of which are very rare, was " Printed for James Roberts," an eminent printer, who was Master of the Stationers Company, 1729–1731, and, as appears from the name in the tail-piece of St. Mark's Gospel, the ornaments were designed by F. (presumably Francis) Hoffman, an engraver of repute resident in England at this date. The work was dedicated to Peter, Lord King, formerly a student at the first Exeter Academy, and the author of a critical history of the Apostles' Creed, whose mother was a cousin of John Locke. He probably assisted in financing the production, since it was not published by subscription, as Mace's Sermons were, and cost only 8s. 6d. (two volumes, 1,060 pages). With a salary of £50 a year, Mace could hardly have commanded the services of men like

James Roberts and Francis Hoffman. The Greek type, an antique type, is peculiarly pleasing, and the translation contains some odd works, on which Wright's Dialect Dictionary throws no light. It was probably printed abroad. In his latest work, *The Text of the Greek Bible*, 1937, Sir Frederick Kenyon pays a belated tribute to Mace. He couples him with Edward Wells, and says: " Both of these editors introduced many emendations which have been accepted by modern criticism, but in their own day their work had no effect." [1]

A number of volumes possessing bibliographical features of some importance are noted elsewhere for other reasons. A few are worth a word or two.

Drayton's *Poly-Olbion*, 1613, contains a note signed " Isaac Moreton Wood, Feast of All Saints, 1845 ": " The author of the Illustrations attached to the end of each song, and signed at the conclusion of the preface ' From the Inner Temple ' is the great Selden, which I discovered from a note in an antique History of Cheshire Gentry, and word for word as given in *Poly-Olbion*, Page 181, Lines 7, 8, 9."

A long MS. note in Latin, dated " Pitcomb, Feb. 21, 1743/4," is prefixed to the third edition (1522) of the Greek Testament by Erasmus discussing this and earlier editions.

Fulke's *Text of the New Testament Translation out of the vulgar Latine by the Papists . . . whereunto is added the Translation out of the original Greek* 1617 contains a valuable bibliographical note on the various editions of the book.

Camden's *Remaines* (1623), formerly in the libraries of Eustace Strickland and Charles Wellbeloved, has a MS. supplement of epitaphs and a sketch. Of Camden's *Britannia* there are three editions, the third (1590), fourth (1594), and Gibson's Translation (folio, 1695). John Barlow's *Exposition of the Second Epistle of the Apostle Paul to Timothy the First Chapter* (1625) contains a note by H. J. Morehouse: " This work is extremely scarce, being the only known copy to exist. It was unknown to Watson or Crabtree in their edition of the *History of Halifax*. According to Lowndes, John Barlow printed a second edition (this the first not being mentioned) folio (1632) entitled *Exposition of the First and Second Epistles of Timothy, with a Discourse of Spiritual Stedfastness and Five Sermons."* John Barlow did not earn a notice in the *Dictionary of National Biography*.

---

[1] See Art. "An almost forgotten pioneer in New Testament Criticism" by the writer, *Hibbert Journal*, July, 1939.

Vox Piscis, Or The Book-Fish. Containing Three Treatises which were found in the belly of a Cod-fish in Cambridge Market, on Midsummer Eve last. Anno Domini 1626 is attributed by the editors to John Frith (1503–1533), but by Anthony Wood in *Athenae Oxonienses* to Richard Tracy (d. 1569), dated 1540, and said to have been dedicated to Richard Cromwell. Our copy, in the original binding, contains three numbered blank pages, and a bibliographical note in pencil. It was formerly in the famous Bibliotheca Heberiana, the great collection formed by Richard Heber (1773–1833).

One of our first editions of Sir Thomas Browne, *Pseudoxia Epidemica* (1646) has a note by a contemporary hand, who may be the writer who signs himself " T. Tatty ": " There are two other editions 4to, one in 1672 enlarg'd with *Religio Medici* . . . the other, I suppose, sent forth ye same year, but without *Religio,* enlarged with *Hydrotaphia* and *Cyrus' Garden.*" The title-page also bears the inscription " Henry Thomson, Penrith, 1800."

The Humble Petition of the Commissioners of the Generall Assembly of the Kirke of Scotland, 1642, has " Commons " for " Commissioners " on the title-page, and is corrected in a contemporary hand.

Of five tracts by Francis Cheynell, one, *The Rise, Growth and Danger of Socinianism,* 1643, was formerly in the possession of Henry Oxenden (or Oxinden), the poet (1609–1690), and bears his signature " Henrie Oxinden." Another, *Chillingworthi Novissima, Or The Sicknesse, Heresy, Death and Buriall of William Chillingworth* (quarto, 1644) is described in a quotation from John Locke as " one of the most villainous books that were ever printed." In five pages of MS. corrections by Alexander Gordon of the life of Cheynell in the *Dictionary of National Biography,* the date given for this book, 1643, is thus corrected: —" The date is 1644. Wood, followed by Calamy, gives 1643, but, if so, it meant 1644, present reckoning. Watt says there was an edition 1645 8vo. I only know the 1644 4to, and the 1725 8vo."

Jeremy Taylor's *Liberty of Prophesying* (1647) contains engravings by W. Holl of Taylor and Barrow, and a print entitled " The Reformation," showing the great Reformers standing round a table on the centre of which is a lighted candle. Luther with an open Bible at one end, the Pope, the Dragon, and two Roman ecclesiastics are at the other. The Roman quartet are vainly endeavouring to extinguish the light, and the legend is " We cannot blow it out."

In Oliver Heywood's *Life in God's Favour* (1679), Morehouse has written: " The original editions of several published works of the Rev. Oliver Heywood are now very scarce. When the Rev. Joseph Hunter compiled *The Life of Mr. Heywood* in 1842 he failed to be able to meet with more than one of the books, viz. *Heart Treasure*, etc., printed in 1667. None of Mr. Heywood's publications are to be found in the British Museum, although they are said to be seventeen in number. He had, therefore, only Vint's reprinted edition for reference. The Rev. Dr. Fawcett, of Halifax, having erected a printing-press of his own at Brierley Hall, where he then resided, reprinted, or professed to do so, one of Mr. Heywood's works, entitled *Life in God's Favour,* in which, however, he took the unwarrantable liberty of making alterations in the text, which the editor of Mr. Heywood's works observes ' cannot with strict propriety be called a republication.' Notwithstanding this, Mr. Vint himself also made considerable alterations, omissions, and additions to that same work! He informs us that he took the liberty of ' substituting Dr. Fawcett's paraphrase instead of the original as the concluding meditation.' Both Mr. Vint and Dr. Fawcett have excluded the *Sacred Poems* of George Herbert at the conclusion of this work. We cannot but condemn this heartless officiousness. It is evident that Herbert was a favourite poet whose writings charmed and warmed the heart of good Mr. Heywood. He divided this work into thirteen chapters, Mr. Vint has divided it into ten." In Heywood's *Baptismal Bonds Renewed,* Morehouse writes: " In this original edition of *Baptismal Bonds Renewed,* printed 1687, which is now very scarce, Mr. Vint, the editor of the reprint of Mr. Heywood's works, professes to have corrected numerous typographical errors, but he does not state why he expunges from it the beautiful poem by his favourite, George Herbert, on Obedience. A modern historian describes Vint's edition of Heywood's *Whole Works* as " unsatisfactory." [1]

A Brief History of the Unitarians, Called also Socinians. Printed in the Year 1687 contains a note by Alexander Gordon. " In this book the term Unitarian first occurs on a title-page. The writer of the Four Letters was Stephen Nye (1648?–1719). ' The Friend,' called also (p. 167) ' the publisher' was Thomas Firmin (1632–1697). The Writer of the appended letters was Henry Hedworth. This copy belonged to Robert Spears (1825–1899)."

In John Clendon's *Treatise on the Word* " Person," 1710, we

---

[1] E. Axon. Life of John Angier—pub. 1937.

read: "This book was suppressed and is very scarce. The Epistle to the Reader ought to precede the first Dedication (that to Lord Cooper). The Table of Contents and Errors are inserted in this copy."

Of David Hume's *Dissertations* (12mo, 1757) there are two copies, one with the Dedication to Home the clergyman-dramatist, and one without. Hume's editors, T. H. Green and T. H. Grose, remark: "At the time when the *Dissertations* were printing, Hume was in ecstasies over the merit of ' Douglas,' and wrote a Dedication to Home, but before the volume appeared he withdrew it for fear of endangering Home's prospects in the Kirk. Shortly afterwards Home resigned his living, and Hume directed that the Dedication should be restored. It is in some copies and not in others."

A volume containing *A Layman's Sermon in Defence of Priestcraft,* n. date, and *Some Thoughts concerning Virtue and Happiness* (1720) is inscribed " Capel Lofft 20 Aug. 1792," and attributed by him to " Nettleton." H. J. Morehouse has prefaced a long note to this book and a still longer one (partly repeating the first) to the second edition of the latter of the two treatises which was published in 1736. As Nettleton has not been honoured with a place in the *Dictionary of National Biography,* extracts from these notes may fitly introduce him. " The Tracts here bound together were published anonymously. The latter, however, were well known to have been written by Thomas Nettleton, physician, of Halifax. A second edition was printed in 1736 which was considerably enlarged, and the title somewhat changed: *A Treatise on Virtue and Happiness*—and yet without the author's name."

"The Rev. John Watson, the historian of the parish of Halifax, in his *Temple of Fame* gives a brief notice of this work. But of *A Layman's Sermon* we do not find any notice in contemporary writers. It is, therefore, doubtful whether its author was publicly known. It certainly was unknown to Mr. Watson, or that it emanated from Halifax. In the search for these ephemeral publications he seems to have bestowed great care. These tracts would seem to have been in the possession of Capel Lofft, Esq., of Troston Hall, in Shropshire (the patron and friend of the author of *The Farmer's Boy*), who has recorded on the title-page that they were written by " Nettleton." A previous owner was " H. Kendall," dated 1739. I find that a Mr. Kendall was Presbyterian minister at Elland (?) for a short time before Dr. Nettleton's death, and that the Kendalls of Shropshire were related to the Nettletons, and that the doctor's grand-daughter, Rebecca Wood, who survived her brothers, lived with her relatives, the Kendalls, in Shropshire. *A Layman's Sermon* is stated to have been "preached to a Private Congregation in 1733" and "occasioned by a Sermon on the Duty of the People to their Pastors." Beyond the London publisher, no name is given. Being dedicated to "the Priests of all Denominations," probably the doctor found it prudent to exercise extreme caution in the distribution of this pamphlet, which, though it contains no special reference to his own district, might have been resented by the pastors to whom it relates with something like modern "boycotting." "The Rev. Mr. Bourne, then Vicar of Halifax, seems to have been distinguished in his sermons for fulsome adulation of loyalty and passive obedience. It would, therefore, appear that the secret had been carefully kept in the families to which it had originally been entrusted till long after the time when it would have ceased to afford annoyance."

"It is stated in Chadwick's *Life of Daniel Defoe* that Defoe resided for a time in the town of Halifax about the latter part of the reign of Queen Anne, when he became acquainted with Dr. Nettleton of that town, and also with the Rev. Nathaniel Priestley, then (1696–1748) minister of the Presbyterian Chapel, Northgate-end. Doubtless their political creeds might to a large extent be in harmony. Dr. N. was a man of liberal views both civil and religious, and of warm and generous sympathies." In the second of the volumes named above, Morehouse gives the genealogy of Nettleton, a brief summary of his life, and particulars of his scientific pursuits. Some of these were "communicated to Dr. Jurin, of the Royal Society, and afterwards printed in the Society's Transactions. Amongst these is the record of Nettleton's inoculation for smallpox of sixty-one persons forty years before the discovery of vaccination by Dr. Edward Jenner. "A later edition of the *Treatise on Virtue and Happiness,* surreptitiously printed, was attributed to William Nettleton M.D., F.R.S." Morehouse also gives extracts from the Diary of Dr. Jessop, of Holmfirth, with whom Nettleton was intimate, concluding: "Dr. Nettleton was very much lamented. He was the author of a *Treatise concerning Virtue and Happiness.* He was born on the 4th of Nov., 1652, and died on the 10th of Jany., 1741, so that he was aged 89 years." The life of Capel Lofft, a previous owner of these volumes, is in the D.N.B.

Pope's *Dunciad* (2nd ed., 1729) contains a note describing it as "the First Complete Edition, The First with the Prolegomena and Notes, and also the First in which the poets' names, who are satirised in it, are given in full."

Birch's *Life of Tillotson* (1752) contains two pages of notes " from Dr. Birch's Memorandums," including a copy of a letter from Thomas Herring, Archbishop of Canterbury, and at the end of the book are printed the additions which appear in the second edition, published 1753.

In a volume containing *A Letter to the Rev. Richard Eliiott* (anon., 1792) and *A Letter addressed to the Rev. W. Moorhouse* (1792), by T. Smart, we are introduced by Morehouse to a humble Unitarian author not elsewhere noticed. "The two following Tracts were written and printed by Mr. Thomas Smart while he was engaged as a journeyman printer with Mr. Joseph Brook, Printer, Huddersfield, with whom he continued for many years. He remained through life a firm and consistent Unitarian Christian though at that time there was no Unitarian place of worship in the town. I knew him intimately in his latter years, and to him I am indebted for the gift of these Tracts. He died November 22, 1846, aged 75."

One of our editions of the *Letters of Junius* (two volumes, 1794) has two title-pages to each volume, bearing respectively the dates 1797 and 1794. The first volume is also numbered Vol. II on its first title-page.

A fine quarto edition of *Lucretius* (1815) contains a note to the effect that " the whole impression was for private distribution, but only twenty-five copies were printed on L.P. like this. The edition has escaped the notice of Dr. Dibdin in his last edition of his work on the Classics."

Another quarto edition of Lucretius *De Rerum Natura* (two volumes, 1725), we are told, is number 333 of an edition of 820, and is signed by the editor " Sigebert Havercamp " (1683–1742) and by the publisher " Jansonius Van Der Aa."

In *Memoirs of the Family of Grace* (1823), by Sheffield Grace, it is said: " Only six copies on extra size page, printed for particular persons."

The Worthies of Yorkshire and Lancashire, by Hartley Coleridge, published in 1833 by F. Bingley, Leeds, with whom the author was then in residence, is the first edition, and on the first page are the words " end of Vol. I." It was published in three numbers, June, 1832, October, 1832, and March, 1833. A note by William Rayner Wood, dated " Sept. 20, 1860 " runs: " This is an incomplete work, three numbers only having been published. My father ordered it as an act of kindness to a gentleman in Manchester of decayed fortune, Mr. Joe Buckley, who was employed to solicit subscriptions."

Unitariorum in Anglia, Historiae, et Status Praesentis Brevis Expositio (1821) was drawn up, "ut apud exteros quoque labores et consilia innotescant." It is probably the last instance of the employment by English Unitarians of Latin—the scholars' *lingua franca*—in order to spread abroad a knowledge of their movement in England. Its composition was doubtless inspired by their introduction to Hungarian Unitarianism in the previous year by John Kenrick, then a student in Germany, who communicated to *The Monthly Repository* a lengthy note on the subject.

A curious book, printed for private circulation, 500 copies, 1854, *Notes and Materials for an Adequate Biography of the Celebrated Divine and Theosopher William Law, comprising an Elucidation of the Scope and Contents of the Writings of Jacob Bohme,*[1] contains opposite the preface the words in MS. "Work of Reference. For the Study of prepared Readers of 35 years of age and upwards. To be previously corrected by the pen after the Copy deposited in British Museum, Bodleian, Oxford, Bristol Library." Other libraries are named in an inserted printed note, dated April, 1861. The margins are crowded with MS. notes, and many passages erased. According to a MS. note based on the text, "the book began to be printed Nov. 1847, was resumed Feby. 1851 and again July 1853. A copy was given to the British Museum, 13 Feb. 1856, the year printed on the back of the book, and a second copy, 3 August 1859." A MS. note on page 237, referring to the printing of books of Mystical Divinity, says: "This and much more glorious results should flow from the proposed establishment of Theosophic Colleges to consist at first of six or seven students selected by a holy extatic(*sic*), a fully regenerated Theosopher (in his magnetic sleep) out of numerous candidates supposed to be adapted for it. . . . " There is no record of the foundation of these colleges.

Unitarian scholars, who were the first in England to recognise the superiority of Griesbach's New Testament text to that of the *Textus Receptus* and to publish translations of it, were also the first to adopt Tischendorf's text after his discovery in 1858 of the *Codex Sinaiticus*. Tischendorf's eighth edition of the New Testament (1865) first took account of this discovery. Robert Ainslie (1803–1876), Unitarian minister of Brighton, straightway broke with the tradition of the Griesbach text in his translation of 1869. The order of the books follows that

---

[1] This book, by Christopher Walton, is said by Dr. Rufus M. Jones (*Spiritual Reformers*) to be "a volume of great value to the student of Boehme."

of the *Codex Sinaiticus,* and the titles, paragraphs, numbering of chapters and verses are those of Tischendorf. The preface gives an account of the discovery of the famous manuscript and of previous English translations of the Greek Testament, noting some of the principal changes in this version as compared with the Authorised Version. A copy of it is in the Library, which also contains Ainslie's own copy of Tischendorf, with his bookplate and that of his son-in-law, Sir John Russell Reynolds Bart., president of the Royal College of Physicians. It is interleaved, and contains in manuscript much of Ainslie's translation, though not exactly in the form in which it was printed, the most quaint expressions, however, being in both the MS. and the published edition. The reference to the tongue in James III.6 has long puzzled translators. The A.V. runs: " It setteth on fire the course (R. V. wheel) of nature." Daniel Mace (1729) rendered it: " It can blast whole assemblies." Of modern translations, Weymouth has " sets the whole course of our lives on fire," and Moffatt, " setting fire to the round circle of existence." Ainslie has a homely rendering: " It setteth on fire the circle of our family," and in his prefatory remarks observes: " I believe it to be an accurate translation, it is common sense—it is a matter of fact, and of universal experience, and presents to us a truth whose power is witnessed in daily life." Again, in Titus II.3, the aged women are bidden be " in behaviour as becometh holiness, not devils." The translation enjoyed little vogue, but is by no means worthless. " As a translator," says its author, " I know nothing of Theology. I have no theological system to uphold." The statement cannot be refuted from his translation.

Occasionally a minister lent sermons to a friend, with the result that *Discourses by the late Rev. T. Kenrick* (two volumes, 1805), as his son informs us in a Memoir of John Kentish, contain two by him. Kentish had lent them to his friend at Exeter " at a time when he was much oppressed by the business of the Academy, and having been copied by Kenrick were supposed by the editors to be his."

IV—Historical and Biographical Notes

ERTAIN previous owners of books in the Library displayed great anxiety to assure the recognition of their rights of ownership. A volume of *Homilies on the Book of Samuel,* in Latin (1554) bears the signature of the presumably original owner dated 1597. This has been crossed out by the next proud possessor, who writes after "liber" and the defaced signature, "at nunc Johannis Ashworthii 1609." A "Breeches Bible" (1610) with Sternhold-Hopkins Psalms appended (1614) has the inscription "James Barrett, his Book." Not content with this, he adds immediately beneath a second signature the words "his thoe troo owner of this Book 1720." Alas, the Barrett family, if it survived, did not treasure the volume as James did, for the next page is a register of the births of a family named "Love" from March 26, 1791, to March 30, 1840, and no connection with the Barretts is claimed.

Calvin's Commentary on the Epistles (Geneva two volumes, 1565) bears the autograph "Leonellus Ducatus" on the title-page. This is identified in a MS. letter by Sir E. Duckett Bart. as the signature of his ancestor, Lionel Duckett (1651–1693), M.P. for Calne. The book is also signed by "Richard Chenevix Trench, Elm Lodge, 1833," Archbishop of Dublin.

Amphitheatrum Aeternae Providentiae Divino-Magicum, by Julius Caesar Voss (Lyons, 1615) contains a note of the author's birth in 1585 and death by burning in 1619, with an extract from Chalmers' Dictionary relating to the volume.

Peacham's *Compleat Gentleman* (4th ed., 1634) bound with the *Gentleman's Exercise* (1634) was formerly in the possession of John Evelyn, the Diarist, and, as his MS. note says, was purchased by him in 1637 when he was a student at Balliol College, Oxford. It contains his autograph, notes on the text, and various pencil marks. Some of these have been discussed by the Rev. A. W. Fox, in *A Book of Bachelors* (1899), dedicated to Alexander Gordon. "In his chapter on poetry, Peacham's list of Elizabethan poets is so incomplete that Evelyn adds thereto such names as those of "Shakespeare, Drayton, Ben Johnson (sic), Sherley (sic), Beaumont, and Fletcher *cum aliis.*" "He designedly omits the great poets who were living in his day, in the not unreasonable confidence that every one would be familiar with their works."[1] When Peacham says of Tacitus (p. 47), "Hee doth in part speake most pure and excellent English, by the industry of that most learned and judicious Gentleman; whose long labour and infinite charge in a farre greater worke, have wonne him the love of the most learned," Evelyn identifies the "Gentleman" in question as "Sir Henry Saville," and to the reference to the practice of Rubens "having some good historian or Poet read to him while he is at worke" Evelyn adds on the margin others who did the same, including "Sir Anthony Vandyke." The diarist gives also notes on the rarity of books mentioned in the text, and explanations of terms used by his author. On the passage (p. 75), which quotes Scaliger's story of a flea "kept daintily in a box, which fed on 'his mistress's white hand,'" Evelyn remarks on some authority known to himself, "one presented to Queen Elizabeth."[2]

A Compleat Collection of the Lives, Speeches, etc., of Those Persons lately Executed, by a Person of Quality (1661) contains the note: "Edward Harrington, his book, the gift of my dear mother Katharine Harrington, bought in January 1660/1." "I began to read this book on Thursday, being 7th March 1660/1." The writer was a relative of James Harrington, author of *Oceana,* of which a folio is in the Library (1758), containing a copy of "A Letter from the London Revolution Society addressed to the 'Society of the Friends of the Constitution at Poictiers,' dated Jany. 30, 1792," which refers to *Oceana.*

Carver's *Discourse of the Terrestrial Paradise* (1666) has a MS. preface by H. J. Morehouse. "The Rev. Marmaduke Carver, the author of this book, was Rector of the Parish of Harthill. Here he is supposed to have composed this work on the site of the terrestrial paradise, which," says the Rev. Joseph Hunter, "was held in high esteem by his contemporaries, and of which, the reader, to whom the original work is not easily accessible, may find an epitome in *Synopsis Criticorum* of his countryman Poole." . . . "Mr. Carver was buried in the

---

[1] A Book of Bachelors, p. 24.
[2] Ibid.

Minster at York with an inscription over his grave in which we have an allusion, rather quaint, to the curious and difficult subject to which he had directed his learned enquiries. He died in 1665." Marmaduke is not in the *Dictionary of National Biography*. Poole's *Synopsis*, five volumes folio, 1666–1676, is in the Library.

In Scapula's *Lexicon Graeco-Latinum* (1637) a note by Dr. Lant Carpenter runs: "A copy of this edition of Scapula, in somewhat better condition, sold at Mr. Johnson's sale (Exeter) for £1 10s. 6d., and sold immediately after for £4 4s., and again for £4 14s. 6d. In Priestley's Catalogue, 1817, it is put at £6 16s. 6d."

A manuscript note, three pages in length, in the first volume of *Morning Exercises at Cripplegate*, consisting of Sermons by the ejected of 1662, indicates the origin of the discourses, many of which were delivered at seven o'clock in the morning, and carefully marks the work of the editors, whose names are given.

The *History* of Polybius, Greek and Latin, is the editio : of 1549, printed at Basel, which first gave extracts from Books VI–XVIII of the original. It contains numerous manuscript notes, and was formerly the property of Nathaniel Tomkins B.D. (d. 1681), a high-churchman, prebendary of Worcester, ejected by the Puritans, but surviving until the Restoration.

Stillingfleet's *Answer to Cressy* (1675) was apparently in the same family for 160 years. It is signed " Samuel Hext, 30 June, 1675 " and "John H. Hext, 1835." Doddridge's *Practical Discourses* (1742) is signed by " Benjamin Wood, May 10, 1743," and " George William Wood, 1809," and remained in the family until 1926, a period of 183 years.

The Censures of the Church Revived. In the Defence of a Short Paper published by the First Classis within the Province of Lancaster (1659) was the property of " R. Brook Aspland, Hackney," who acquired it " December 10, 1868," and describes it as "a curious volume (illustrating the religious history of Lancashire) long sought for." He has prefaced it with a long manuscript introduction, giving its origin and history, as also of the *Excommunicatio excommunicata* to which it is an answer. He has also provided it with an Index of Names, adding: "Of many of the persons whose names are in the Index opposite, notices may be found in the Index appended to the Civil War Tracts (Chetham Society, Vol. I), also in the Diaries of H. Newcome and Adam Martindale." The volume was marked by the bookseller " Very rare."

In not a few books the manuscript notes by H. J. Morehouse have been corrected by Alexander Gordon, *e.g.* in a volume of *Tracts* (1655), and an *Address* attributed to " Bidle " is said to be by " Jeremiah Ives."

Three volumes of Milton's *Works* (quarto, 1698) contain the autograph of Richard Milnes, of Chesterfield (1636–1706), a contemporary for thirty-eight years of the poet. " From Robert, the eldest son of Richard Milnes," we are told, " descended Richard Monckton Milnes, created in 1863 Lord Houghton," the well-known man of letters. A genealogical table at the end of the volume traces the connection of the Milnes and the Wood families. From a member of the last-named family the volume passed into the Library.

Roma Racoviana et Racovia Romana (1702), by William Jameson, contains MS. excerpts from the records of Glasgow University from 1692 to 1722 relating to the author, furnished to Alexander Gordon, February–March, 1879, when he was at work upon *The Sozzini and Their School* for the *Theological Review*. One is worth reproducing: " Mr. William Jameson who had been born blind yet having been educate at this University hath atteaned to great learning and particularly is well skilled in history, both civill and ecclesiastical, appointed him to ' have a public prelection of civill history once a week ' in Latin in the Common Hall. A salary of £33 6s. 8d. was afterwards granted to him out of the archiepiscopal revenues of Glasgow, and this he held till his death, apparently in 1721." The book shows the writer's knowledge of the *Fratres Poloni* and of the old *Unitarian Tracts*. He has been given a place in the *Dictionary of National Biography*. An earlier volume by the same writer is also in the Library.

The Occasional Papers (1716–1719) were formerly owned by Joshua Toulmin (1746–1853). Toulmin writes in Vol. I: " The writers of *The Occasional Papers* were Brown, Avery, Grosvenor, Wright, Evans, Earl, and Lowman—the initials forming the word " Bagweell." The last " l " was not deciphered to my friend Mr. Watson, of Bridgewater, who gave me this information. This note is signed and dated " April 26, 1792." Later he added: " Lardner is said to be the second 'l.' " In the preface to his edition of Neal's *History of the Puritans* (1793), Toulmin gives six of the above names, and in a letter to the *Protestant Dissenter's Magazine* (1798) the contributions of five writers, with the remark, " there is every reason to credit the accuracy of my information, as it comes from the lips of the late Dr. Flexman, through my deceased friend, the Rev. Thomas Watson, of Bridgwater." Writing, finally, to the *Monthly Repository* (1813) he gives all the names, including that of Lardner. All the writers were men of some note in their day. Jabez Earle was a witty centenarian Presbyterian divine, who is said to have spoken of his three wives as " the world, the flesh, and the devil."

The Library, Or Moral and Critical Magazine (1761–1762), edited by Dr. Joseph Jeffries, was formerly in the library of the Rev. John Ralph, minister at Halifax, 1767–1795, who has identified in MS. notes a few of the contributors. This volume is very rare, and the writer consulting it a few years ago found a copy only in King's College Library, Aberdeen.

In Priestley's *Theological Repository* (six volumes, 1768–1772; 1784–1788) the anonymous contributors are identified; *The Mirror,* an Edinburgh periodical (three volumes, 1799–1800), contains a list of 110 articles, identifying their writers; and the *Christian Moderator* (1826–1828) has the names of most writers in it added.

The writers of many anonymous works are written on the title-pages of the Library copies, and the anonymous tracts and pamphlets of one author, in several instances, have been brought together and bound under his name. Thus have been collected, for example, the writings of Arthur Anthony Sykes (1684–1756), the latitudinarian divine of the school of Hoadly, whose pen-names are identified, including the mysterious T.P.A.P.O. A.B.I.T.C.O.S., which are the first letters of the words " The Precentor and Prebendary of Alton Borealis in the Church of Salisbury.

A manuscript volume gives a list of " the writers in the *Monthly Repository,* 1830–1836, " arranged and copied " in 1903 by Alexander Gordon, from a British Museum manuscript written by the daughter of William Johnson Fox, the proprietor and editor of the journal from 1831–1836.

An essay on " Joseph Priestley " in three articles by James Martineau, contributed in 1833, was his first production of importance, which, when reprinted in 1852, was radically revised, its author by that time having thrown off his bondage to the philosophical school in which he was trained at York. It is noteworthy that these three articles were unsigned, though two written by Martineau in 1831 were signed.

In 1834, Martineau contributed an unsigned article on

Bentham's *Deontology,* which still more clearly exhibited his devotion to the school of David Hartley and James Mill. This article is not included in the MS. list by Gordon, and, presumably, was not in that compiled by Miss Fox. A. W. Jackson, in his *Life of James Martineau,* and Gordon, in his *Dictionary of National Biography* article, attribute to Martineau, not this article, but four articles on Bentham's work in the *Christian Reformer* for 1845, apparently being misled by a conversation with Martineau himself. C. B. Upton, however, has conclusively proved (*Life and Letters of James Martineau,* II, 264–6) that the article in the *Monthly Repository* was from Martineau's pen, and Richard Garnett, in the *Life of W. J. Fox* (1910) speaks of its authorship by Martineau as "wrongly contested."

Possibly the fact that these two contributions by Martineau were unsigned, and the authorship of the second unknown to Miss Fox, may suggest his hesitation to avow a wholehearted acceptance of the necessarian and utilitarian philosophy he afterwards so vigorously rejected.

Biographical notes are found in innumerable volumes in the Library. The one in *A Declaration from York,* by Sir Francis Wortley (1642) is almost as long as the tract itself.

The original folio edition, posthumously published, of Bishop Burnet's *History of His Own Time* (two volumes, 1734) was the property of his son. The first volume contains his notes on his father's work collected from other writers. The second volume has the words: "The original Manuscript of both volumes of the History will be deposited in the Cotton Library." The Cotton Library, built up by Sir Robert Bruce Cotton (1571–1631) and his son, Sir Thomas, was presented to the nation in 1700 and transferred to the British Museum in 1753.

Richard Baxter's *True and Only Way of Concord* (1680) is of interest from its associations. It came from the " New Meeting-house, Kidderminster," in the vestry of which Baxter's pulpit, purchased from the authorities of the Parish Church for a trifling sum in 1780, is still preserved. It contains two pages of shorthand notes and the signature " Thos. Tayler." Amongst the numerous works of Baxter in the Library are thirty-six first editions.

In more than one of several volumes of tracts relating to the Revolution of 1688, H. J. Morehouse wrote: " These Tracts belonged to my ancestors, and formed part of a thick volume of Tracts. . . . They have at length come into my possession, and are now divided into small volumes."

The *Works of Tacitus,* four volumes edited by J. G. Gronovius and published by Elzevir in 1672, contains the bookplate of Joseph Smith (1682–1770), British Consul at Venice, and an extract from a letter by C. Godwyn, dated Baliol (*sic*) College, September, 1762, telling of the King's purchase of Smith's collection of books, including "a great number of the scarce first printed editions of the Classics." George III gave £10,000 for these books, and they now form an important part of the King's library in the British Museum. Books acquired subsequently to this purchase were sold by auction in London after Smith's death—the sale occupying thirteen days. This edition of Tacitus formerly belonged to Charles Wellbeloved.

Unlike the detached and disinterested students who now occasionally peruse such works to-day, early readers of sixteenth and seventeenth century theological treatises, being zealous for Romanism or Protestantism, King or Parliament, Uniformity or Toleration, could not refrain from delivering their souls on the book which attracted or repelled them by its political or religious sentiments.

The value of such notes depends usually, but not invariably, on who wrote them. De Quincey, in his literary reminiscences, contrasts Coleridge and Wordsworth in this respect: "Coleridge often spoiled a book, but, in the course of doing this, he enriched that book with many and valuable notes, tossing about him, with lavish profusion, from a cornucopia of discursive reading. . . . Wordsworth rarely, indeed, wrote on the margin of books, and, when he did, nothing could less illustrate his intellectual superiority. The comments were such as might have been made by anybody."

Some of the notes in the Library books, it must be confessed, are like those of Wordsworth; happily others more resemble Coleridge's.

Epistolae Erasmi (Froben, 1521), bearing name and date of owner in 1605, has been carefully read and approved passages underlined. Platina's *De Vita et Moribus Summorum Pontificum* (1529) has been annotated throughout by a contemporary who did not scruple to erase (with marginal corrections) paragraphs and sentences with which he was in disagreement. On the other hand, a collection of *Meditations and Sermons* by Edward Reynolds (1599–1676), a member of the Westminster Assembly, was formerly owned by "R. Riddell," who inserted verses in praise of the author together with some shrewd knocks at Roman doctrine. Treasured for 200 years by one family, the book was given in 1844 by an "affectionate mother" to her daughter.

The one-time owner of Stillingfleet's *Rational Account of the Grounds of the Protestant Religion* (1655) found it impossible to keep his pen still as he followed its argument, and poured out ink copiously on the broad margins of the folio. Touched by a discourse in Izaak Walton's *Life and Sermons of Dr. Sanderson* (1678), another scribe writes: "Q(uery) Is faith to be kept with an enemy? A(nswer) You are not so much to consider to whom as by whom thou hast sworn, and therefore he is found much faithfuller than thou, which believing thee having sworn by the name of God, hast been deceived in you that by that means hast deceived him; though nothing be now more common than so to deceive."

An anonymous *Commentary upon the Epistle to the Hebrews* (folio, 1646), a translation from the Latin of Crellius and Schlichtingius, but not without alterations and additions, is the work of Thomas Lushington, 1589–1661. A former owner has signed his name and date several times "John Roberts, his Booke 1742." Three other owners are apparent; two from the inscription "Mathilda Cullen, Bought at Mrs. Bosberry's Sale, Nov., 1837," and a third from the historical note by Walter H. Burgess, an old student of the College, dated December, 1898, which quotes from a manuscript note by Joshua Wilson, the Independent (1795–1874): "This somewhat rare book is one of the early Socinian publications in England."

In Stephen Lobb's *Growth of Error* (1697), published anonymously, a rare anti-Socinian treatise, a story is told exposing the perfidy of Socinians. Unfortunately, as another MS. note discloses, it is not corroborated by historical research. The difference in value between oral tradition and written evidence is thus made plain. The title-page is inscribed "Richard Duke," and a note by the same hand dated "Bath, May 2, 1720" runs: "At Monpelier in the year 1674 I saw one Mons. Dumount, a Protestant minister, who was deposed for Socinianism. He was first found out by altering ye form of Baptism, wch he administered *Au nom de Père et non du fils et Saint Esprit,* for wch He was prosecuted before the Parliament of Toulouse, and condemned to lose his head, wch he thought to redeem by sacrificing his fair daughter to the President of that Parliament, as was generally reported at Monpelier when I was there. Richard Duke."

In a letter attached to the volume, the Rev. Alexander Gordon M.A. tells a different story, under date " May 5, 1910 ": " Bonet-Maury has referred me to Ph. Corbière's *Hist. de l'Englise Reformée de Montpellier* (1861), from which I learn as follows: Etienne Dumont was born at Pay-l'Evêque, department of Lot, studied at Geneva, was pastor at Graisses duc 1668-9, at Nîmes 1669-79, and therewith at Montpellier 1670-71. But on April 15, 1671, at the Synod of Bas-Languedoc, assembled at Nîmes, he was suspect of Arianism, and after examination was deposed from his pastorate at Montpellier. Whether the above dates show that the Nîmes Reformed were less suspicious, or more tolerant, than those of Montpellier does not appear. However, in 1680, a year of stringent persecution, he ' apostasised from the evangelic faith and got a pension from Louis XIV, on becoming a Roman Catholic.' There is no reference whatever to any prosecution before the Parlement (*i.e.*, High Court) of Toulouse, or to the scandal about his daughter. I incline to imagine that if R. Duke's memory, after 46 years, was accurate, the story was largely due to Montpellier malice in regard to the suspect."

Occasionally the text of a book is discussed or criticised by a scribe. Whitaker's *History of Manchester* (two volumes, 1773) contains a lengthy " memorandum " regarding the Roman Fort at Singleton, described on pp. 237-238, giving in detail an account of the size based on conversation (August 18, 1839) with a man of sixty-seven years of age, who had worked at Singleton thirty-one years, *i.e.* since 1808.

Whitaker is honoured in several notices by Gibbon. In one he says: " The lively spirit of the learned and ingenious antiquarian has tempted him to forget the nature of a question he so *vehemently* debates and so *absolutely* decides! " Yet the point in debate, which Whitaker maintains and Gibbon derides is said by J. B. Bury, the great editor of Gibbon, to be " now generally admitted."

In a collection of Salters' Hall Controversy Tracts formerly in the library of Edward Harwood, already noticed, there is inscribed on the title-page of *A Letter to the Rev. Dr. Waterland, by Philanthropus Oxoniensis* (1722), " Dr. Flexman told me that this was the most sensible Pamphlet in the whole controversy." Roger Flexman (1708-1795) was remarkable for his historical knowledge. " Happening one day," says Boswell, " to mention Mr. Flexman, a Dissenting minister, with some Compliments to his exact memory in chronological matters, the Doctor replied: 'Let me hear no more of him, Sir, That is the fellow who made the Index to my *Rambler,* and set down the name of Milton thus: Milton, *Mr.* John.'"

In Volume II of *Biographica Classica,* 2nd ed., 1750, a contemporary has written opposite the title-page: "By the Rev. Dr. Edward Harwood of Hyde Street, Bloomsbury, who also published 'A View of the Various Editions of the Greek and Roman Classics' in 1789. He is now alive, May 1st, 1794, very old and so very poor that he sold his Library in January 1793." The facts are that Harwood died January 14, 1794, and that the volume named was published in 1775, 2nd ed. 1778, 3rd ed. 1782, and 4th ed. 1790. Unfortunately the poverty of this scholar in old age is indisputable.

"*Sermons on Various Subjects* by the late Reverend Mr. John Holland. In Two Volumes 1753 " is signed " Mary Holland 1754," and contains the following manuscript note: "Mary Holland, whose signature appears on the title-page, was the daughter of Mr. John Holland of Mobberley, and sister of the author of the Book. She was married in 1758 to the Revd. William Turner, afterwards of Wakefield, and was the Mother of the Revd. William Turner, afterwards of Newcastle-on-Tyne, and of John Turner, of Bolton, my Father. J. Aspinall Turner." The writer of the note, a well-known Unitarian, was M.P. for Manchester in two parliaments.

The Apology of Benjamin Mordecai (quarto, 1771, 3, 4) by Henry Taylor, "one of the last of the Anglican divines of the Clarkean school," was the author's own copy, and includes his corrections, voluminous notes, and index. It was formerly the property of Alexander Gordon, the biographer of Taylor in the *Dictionary of National Biography.*

One of the copies of Thomas Belsham's *Life of Theophilus Lindsey* (1723–1808) is in two volumes, interleaved, and contains also Belsham's Funeral Sermon for Lindsey (1808) and that for wife (1812), the latter given, February 12, 1812, by the author to John Disney D.D. (1746–1816), who had married the half-sister of Mrs. Lindsey. Disney, whose bookplate and initials are in the volumes, has written copious notes throughout, correcting the laudatory expressions of Belsham, his successor at Essex Street Chapel, London, especially those relating to Mrs. Lindsey, has identified and expanded references to persons alluded to or named in the biography, provided an index to expressions and statements to which he took exception, and, what is more important, has greatly enlarged the catalogue of

Lindsey's publications given by Belsham by adding the "Fugitive Pieces," with their signatures, contributed by his brother-in-law to various journals in 1771, 1772, 1773, *i.e.* before Lindsey became a Unitarian. The volume passed into the hands of Robert Brook Aspland (1805–1869), who also added, from manuscript and printed sources, biographical and historical notes, including letters of Lindsey. From one note we learn that the letters of Lindsey, now in Dr. Williams' library, were in 1861 in the possession of Mr. J. A. Turner M.P., whose grandfather was the Rev. William Turner, the recipient of the letters in question. Following the example of Disney, Aspland initialed his notes, and inserted plates previously published in periodicals. All the notes are carefully documented. Even when ample allowance is made for the lack of cordiality between Mrs. Disney and her half-sister, which inspired some of Disney's corrections and additions, it is safe to say that this unique volume affords the fullest view attainable of the life and labours of the first minister of Essex Street Chapel.

The Loyal Miscellany. Consisting of Several Sermons, and Other Tracts and Essays, by John Du Pont (two volumes, 1751), was the work of one unnoticed in the *D.N.B.* H. J. Morehouse gives in MS. an account of the author, a bibliographical note, and an extract from the preface. The first and last are not without interest. "The Rev. John Dupont was vicar of Aysgarth in the North Riding of Yorkshire. His ancestors were French refugees, who fled to England in consequence of the Revocation of the Edict of Nantes, for their adherence to Protestantism. . . . Mr. Dupont was a warm supporter of the House of Hanover, during the Scotch Rebellion in 1745. He published Sermons and Tracts on that occasion, and in consequence of his active exertions in the cause, it would seem that his life was in some danger from his enemies. . . . " In the preface he states: " As the storm still continued to rage with uncontrolled violence, I preached and printed a Sermon upon the Rebellion, when a party of that misguided and infatuated multitude was within a few miles of my parish; and I have just reason to think it so nettled the Pretender's partizans in the neighbourhood, that a sturdy Fellow was sent soon after to my House, who threatened me with having my throat cut and being afterwards hung up at my door, with a view of intimidating me from attempting anything further in the Defence of my country. . . . "

In two of three volumes of Political and Ecclesiastical Tracts (1628–1689) are numerous business memoranda by former owners, Thomas and Samuel Goodier, of Newton, dated 1720 on, chiefly relating to sales of hides. Volume II contains an I.O.U. for £10 by "Samuel Goodier to Jarge Wooley," attested by "John Gee, Curet of Wodhed." This is followed by nine pages of MS. political verse entitled "A Dream of the Caball," beginning:

> "As t'other night in bed I thinking lay
> How I my rent should to my landlord pay . . . "

The Annals of the Reign of George the Third, by John Aikin (two volumes, 1820), was formerly the property of the Duke of Sussex. It contains his book-plate and many autograph notes. Here are three: —Commenting on the passage of the Stamp Act (1765), Aikin said: "During this period His Majesty had been labouring under an indisposition, since generally understood to have been of the same nature with that which has so deeply affected the latter years of his reign." On an inserted leaf the royal scribe disputes the statement.

"This is a great mistake, for I heard my mother say that the King caught a cold, and it passed upon his lung from being neglected. He was thus very frequently, and from the impossibility of bleeding him in the left arm, the victim of the fever had such a swelling round the orifice of the right arm that in a moment when it was necessary to repeat the bleeding, Hawkins, the surgeon, declared he did not dare to attempt it. Sir Edward Wilmot, the physician, called out immediately, 'Peynelt, take out your lancet, if you are worth anything in your profession, you should know how the veins lie. The king can but die, but this may save him.' Within a very few minutes after His Majesty opened his eyes, and, smiling at Peynelt, said in a low voice, 'My good friend, I thank you. I heard all and prayed you might succeed. . . . My mother always said that my Father owed his life to the courage and dexterity of Peynelt Hawkins.' "

Aikin's view of the character of the King's illness was that of Smollett in the fifth volume of his *Continuation of the Complete History of England.* This volume is extremely rare, and there is a tradition that nearly all the copies of it were destroyed in 1765. The greatest secrecy was preserved concerning this illness of King George, and the question remains for historians to determine whether the book disappeared because Smollett's statement about it was correct, or because it was incorrect, as the Duke of Sussex says the similar statement in Aikin's history was.

On page 262 Aikin describes the Gordon Riots of 1780, and speaks of the irresolution of the ministry. The king's son adds:

"It was the firmness of King George the Third which put an end to this frightful movement. The Lord Mayor was timid—the ministry puzzled, and never would act. The King declared he would take the office of First Magistrate as well as of King, and gave the order for troops. On the 6th or 7th of June (I cannot just mark the day), after Lord Rockingham had spoken in Council with great appreciation of the firmness of the King and explicitly said that it was the only thing to be done, his Lordship was attacked by someone of Lord George Gordon's mob in the street. He was so very much alarmed that he came to the Queen's House and begged to see the King. His Majesty was at Dinner, but immediately went to his private room, into which he ordered Lord Rockingham to be admitted, whom he found in a great state of hysteria, pale, and with very anxious countenance. The King's first words were 'Now what has happened, my Lord?' 'Sir, everything that is bad must be expected from the victories of the lower orders, and I have reflected that this is the moment for your Majesty to declare yourself a despotic monarch.' The King instantly replied, 'I desire, my Lord, you will not tax us. . . . You are ill. You are not able to stand. Listen to what I have to say. My Lord, go home, go to bed, and don't utter a syllable of what has passed. A good night's rest will prove that your nerves were much affected to-day, and you will do me the honour to try soon to forget what you said this evening.'"

The statement (p. 333) respecting Fox's India Bill, that "His Majesty declared he should deem them who should vote for the Bill not only not his friends but his enemies," is strengthened by the scribe's remark:

"King George sent to Lord Winchester, then His Majesty's favourite, with orders to go immediately to all the Lords of the Bedchamber with the Peers in place at that time to vote against the Bill before Supper to-morrow, for he should otherwise list them as his enemies."

"The result was," said the historian, "that on a decision upon the question of adjournment the ministers were left in the minority of 79 to 87, to which the Duke of Sussex adds, 'Thank God.'"

Summa Universae Theologiae Christianae secondum Unitarios (1787), published anonymously, was written by Michael de

Szent Abraham, Bishop or Superintendent of the Unitarian Churches in Transylvania from 1737–1758. The decree of Joseph II authorising its publication is given in a note. It is indicative of that monarch's generous and broad-minded religious spirit. "The MS. forwarded to the government with the title 'Summa Univ. Theol. etc.' is now returned to the Transylvanian authorities with the remark that its impression is the more readily granted, as besides that this religion is one of those recognised in Transylvania, the tone of tolerant moderation pervading the work may well serve as a model for other religious writings. Signed, Charles, Count Palfy, in accordance with His Majesty's commands."

The hostility towards Unitarians which previously obtained in Austrian official circles may be seen from the fact that this work must have lain in manuscript for nearly thirty years, and was only then published without name.

Milton's work on Christian Doctrine, published posthumously in 1825, edited by C. R. Sumner, is here in Latin and in English. The former volume was once the property of C. C. Bunsen (1791–1860), the German historian, and later of H. L. Mansel (1820–1871), the English philosopher, and bears the bookplate of the one and the signature of the other.

John Keble's *Christian Year* (1874), illustrated by Fr. Overbeck, contains a letter by the author, dated June 17, 1848, to the printer, giving suggestions as to the printing of his sermons. One is "that the name of each Sermon should appear at the top of the page, as in Mr. Newman's Sermons"; another, that "the Preface may go to the Press last, in case I should wish to make any verbal alterations." The volume has an added illustration of Keble College.

Biographical, bibliographical, and historical notes by Alexander Gordon are to be found in most of his former books, and to many is added an index. His MS. index to *Calendar of State Papers*, 1672–1673, published 1897, 1899, 1901, is a bound volume of 267 pages. One note, characteristic of the author, is in a volume of dissenting history: "Bound and presented by A.G., who wishes it were more correct." Another, in *The History and the Litigation and Legislation respecting Presbyterian Chapels and Charities*, by T. S. James (1867) says: "In this copy the print of Evans's List has been revised by the original, and some few corrections made." "Evans's List" refers to a valuable manuscript in Dr. Williams's library. That corrections in this volume were necessary had been demonstrated by John Gordon, father of the corrector, in the year of its publication. All John Gordon's writings collected together by his son are in the Library, including his critical examination of James's partisan treatise, published under the title of Nonconformity and Liberty.

One copy of the *Dictionary of National Biography* is unique. The original edition, with supplementary volumes, it is packed with annotations, additions, corrections, engravings, insertions and illustrations. As Alexander Gordon was one of the two men (the other was Sir Sidney Lee) who contributed to the *Dictionary* from first to last (720 articles containing 778 biographies), his MS. comments and notes, especially those on dissenting authors, are of peculiar value. He indicates, by brackets, editorial additions to his own articles, expressing in the margin his estimate of their worth. In the life of Timothy Manlove, *e.g.*, he corrects the birth date, and characterises the reference to his parentage as " a foolish editorial addition." With the *Dictionary* came also into the Library the files of manuscripts of Gordon's articles, together with data, printed and manuscript, on which they were based.

Copies of *The Records of the Provincial Assembly* (1896) and *Vestiges of Protestant Dissent* (1897), both by Mr. G. Eyre Evans, are interleaved and crowded with notes. So too is Killen's *History of the Presbyterian Church in Ireland* (1886). In older books, Gordon's bibliographical notes are the rule, not the exception. Thus a volume of Irish Presbyterian Sermons, 1736–1749, contains a letter thereon addressed to Gordon, and a query by him sent to *Notes and Queries* relative to the first publication. " Two Sermons by Richard Buffington. Dublin, 1740," said to have been given " before the Scholars at Killead, Anno 1701."

Gordon proves that it cannot have been printed before 1749, nor later than November, 1750—the date of the signature of a former owner—and that the days when the sermons were said to have been preached were a Monday and a Saturday. As he knew no other edition of the sermons, nor anything about the preacher, Gordon suspected the title was " fudge." Both sermons are anti-papal, with scandalous stories of Popes and ecclesiastics, and include many colloquial expressions, some of Scottish origin.

The character of the manuscript notes in a single volume may be illustrated by what is added to one of the copies of Murch's *History of the Presbyterian and General Baptist Churches in the West of England*, 1835.

F

In the section on Bridport, is a letter from James Edwin Odgers to Gordon relating to the origin of the congregation, and giving information additional to the printed word; Gordon's reply, February 17, 1894, dealing with eight points raised by Odgers, and, finally, a letter from H. Shaen Solly, then minister at Bridport, to Odgers, May 10, 1894, to whom Gordon's letter had been sent, including a long extract from the Trust Deed of 1794, and notes on a few other relevant matters.

The copy of the first volume of *The Inquirer* (1842) was the property of Samuel Sharpe (1799–1881), who, in a long MS. note, sketches the foundation and history of the paper down to 1876, with several pages of notes identifying his own contributions to it during that period.

Books in a library are never dead. They reveal the living thoughts of their authors, to which is added, in these manuscript notes of " association copies," precious glimpses of the minds of their readers, speaking to us of thoughts and feelings common to men in all ages, and sometimes, at least, casting fresh light on matters historical, biographical, or bibliographical.

V—Presentation Copies

HARLES Lamb defines a presentation copy as " a copy of a book which does not sell sent you by the author, with his foolish autograph at the beginning of it, for which, if a stranger, he only demands your friendship; if a brother author, he expects from you a book which does sell." Not all the presentation copies in the Library belong to this category, but it would be idle to deny that some probably do. Liberal dissenting divines from 1750 to 1850 appear to have freely exchanged their sermons and pamphlets, and none to have been any the worse for it, since the question of sale did not seriously arise on either side. They were doubtless encouraged in the habit by the practice of District Societies, Provincial Societies, and, at a later date, national organisations, which almost invariably printed their annual sermons.

Manuscript letters in the Library throw some light on the production of printed sermons at the beginning of last century. In 1811 an estimate for printing 450 sermons is given as six guineas, and sermons sold at 1s. or 1s. 6d. each. Their sale, though more considerable than in our day, seldom covered the cost of production. Hence the inducement was ever present to preachers to introduce their discourses to friends and sympathisers at a distance. One note (October 11, 1813) explains, in part at least, the type and format of some sermons in the Library, and proves that publication in country towns had its drawbacks. " My sermon," says the writer, " has at length, after various delays, come from the press. Both the compositor and printer are boys of no education. I had much trouble in correcting the sheets, and though I detected a number of errors, some still remain."

A few laymen, honoured by the receipt of autographed sermons, bound them handsomely in sets. Some of the gifts of one divine to another present in their inscriptions curious problems. A handsome volume labelled " Allin's Works " contains one lengthy tract and three short ones, dated respectively 1849, 1826, 1833, and 1835. The inscription runs: "Presented to the Rev. John Gordon by T. Allin, Sept. 15, 1859." Thomas Allin (1784–1866) was an eminent Methodist minister and John Gordon had begun his ministry as a Methodist. In the book also is a three page letter by Dr. J. Pye Smith, the Independent Tutor, dated "Homerton, May 17, 1850," acknowledging the *Discourses* (1849), and relating how he adopted them as a text-book for his students in the academy. Dr. Pye Smith died in 1851. Eight years later, either Allin enclosed the letter, or both tracts and letter, in the bound volume sent to Gordon, and in either event the latter connects together three ministers, Methodist, Independent, and Unitarian. The book formed part of Alexander Gordon's inheritance from his father.

Occasionally, the gift of sermons to a friend has resulted in a collection in the Library which is complete and rare. Thus all the printed works of Charles Beard LL.D., many of them autographed, are at Summerville, from the sermon printed in 1850 at the beginning of his ministry at Hyde "at the request and expense of the congregation, and for their use alone" to the last posthumous volume published in Liverpool.

Some recipients of presentation copies may even have read them, a thing which Oliver Wendell Holmes said never happened.

One volume of eighteenth century sermons, mainly episcopal, were collected and bound by William Williams, a clergyman of High-Wycombe, Bucks, who to several presented to him added some of his own, correcting the text of many, and to three by well-known Unitarians has added prefatory words on the title-page, which now reads: "Unitarian Doctrines, Sectarian Murmurs, and Ill-Founded Hopes in *Three Discourses by William Enfield, Richard Godwin, and Philip Holland*" (1780).

Sermons, however, are by no means the only works which passed from hand to hand. Two seventeenth century volumes, which passed through the hands of three men of parts, are *Annales Rerum Anglicarum et Hibernicae, Regnante Elizabetha* (two volumes, 1615). They are inscribed by the author, William Camden (1551–1615) as a gift "amoris pignus" to Walter Quin (1575–1634), poet and preceptor to Charles I, and later came into the possession of Sir Philip Warwick (1609–1685), secretary to the unfortunate monarch, and bear his signature on the title-pages of both volumes.

The Two Great Mysteries of the Christian Religion, by G.G. (1653), is the work of Godfrey Goodman (1583–1656). He was Bishop of Gloucester during the Long Parliament, was impeached with Laud in August, 1641, and committed to the Tower, but released on bail after eighteen weeks imprisonment. Appended to the preface, addressed to Oliver Cromwell, is the following note: "This treatise was given to me William Blundell at London in ye year 1653 by my very good friend ye author, and I think it was ye first copy what came from ye press. He dyed about two or three years after ye publication of ye same, and I do well remember what ye weekly newes-book reported yt he dyed a Roman Catholic; wch I have cause to beleeve was true." The writer William Blundell, of Crosby (1620–1698), was a Roman Catholic officer, and an author of works on topography. *The Cavalier's Note Book* (1880), edited by T. E. Gibson from the manuscripts of Blundell at Crosby Hall, is in the Library, together with *The Crosby Records,* also edited by Gibson. The preface to the former indicates that "if the present publication meet with the favour of the public," Gibson intended to publish later the letters of William Blundell. These were published (1933), edited by Margaret Blundell, but including none which passed between the Cavalier and the Bishop. The author remarks, however, on Blundell's handwriting as "small and neat" and on his being "an interested reader of the Press of his time, particularly The Newsbook," edited by Roger Lestrange. In the *Dictionary of National Biography,* Sir Sidney Lee, the biographer of Goodman, does not give the title of *The Two Great Mysteries* exactly as it is found in the Library.

One of seven original editions of the works of James Ussher, Archbishop, *The Reduction of Episcopacie under the Form of Synodical Government* (1656), which was given to Alexander Gordon in 1897, had been "found in a stable in Pembrokeshire." This book played a great, though ineffective, part in the futile negotiations between Presbyterians and Episcopalians after the Restoration of Charles II.

Bacon's *Essayes* (1632) is inscribed "The gift of John Lee 1755." John Lee (1733–1793) was solicitor-general in the Rockingham, and attorney-general in the Portland administrations. He was a personal friend of Priestley and Lindsey. The book was presented to Mrs. Josiah Oates, of Leeds, an ancestor of the "very gallant gentleman," who walked out into the storm to meet death when the Scott expedition to the South Pole was drawing near to its sad fate.

Grotius' *Annales et Historiae* (1658), signed by John Johnstone (1768–1836) and Samuel Parr (1747–1821), was the gift of the latter to the former, his friend and afterwards his biographer. As companions in the Library, there are Field's *Life of Parr* (two volumes, 1826); Barker's *Parriana* (two volumes, 1828); Parr's *Works* (eight volumes, 1826), and numerous volumes containing the signature of "the Whig Johnson," as his friends called him.

The Confession of Faith . . . Composed by the Reverend Assembly of Divines sitting at Westminster (1658) was the gift to the Library of T. L. Marshall (1825–1919), editor of *The Inquirer,* 1856–1887.

The Fanatical History of the Old Anabaptists and the New Quakers (1660) bears this note, written in a beautiful hand: "William David, his book. Given him by his Master the Honble. Sir Charles Kemeys barront. in the year of our Lord 1731."

Owen Felltham's *Resolves* (1635) bears an inscription by Alexander Gordon: "10 Jany. 1883. Given to me by his sister Harriet in remembrance of George Benn, Historian of Belfast, with whom it was a favourite book." George Benn (1801–1882) had been a member of the First Presbyterian Church, Belfast, of which Gordon was then minister. His writings are in the Library.

The Sinner's Hope (1660), sermons by Henry Newcome, the Manchester ejected minister, passed through many hands: "Richard Buerdsell," "Ferdinando Burdsell," "Richard Leason, 1720," "Samuel Davenport, 1764," and finally, "J. G. Robberds, from Mr. Aston, November 3, 1824." "Mr. Aston" was father of John Partington Aston, Unitarian lawyer, and secretary to the trustees of John Owens' Trust for many years. The volume, with many others, was presented to the Library by the widow of J. G. Robberds, minister of Cross Street Chapel, on his death in 1854.

A volume of seventeen sermons, 1669–1707, presents a series of problems. It is prefaced by a manuscript index, dated Anno Domini 1718, and signed "William, My Book," but the first sermon bears the name and date "Jno Summers, Anno Domini 1729," and a statement that the sermon, published 1728, by Thomas Lamplugh, Bishop of Exeter (afterwards Archbishop of York), was the gift of the author to the writer. Another sermon (1702) bears the signature "Thomas Myles' Book." The volume, which came from Northgate End Chapel, Halifax, contains numerous notes on the sermons; in particular, on the doctrine of eternal torments in a sermon preached before Queen Mary, March 16, 1688/9, which comes in for much criticism. Apparently the book, or, at least, the sermons in it, went through more hands than one, and the owners were not in complete theological agreement.

An Enquiry into the Constitution of the Primitive Church, published anonymously (Pt. I, 1691, Pt. II, 1713), is the work of Peter, Lord King, the biographer of John Locke, cousin of his mother. The copy is signed by Job Orton, pupil, assistant, and biographer of Philip Doddridge, and was given to the Rev. Edmund Kell by the Rev. James Scott "October 1814." King's *History of the Apostles' Creed* (2nd ed., 1703) came from the Tenterden Chapel Library, and is signed by Lawrence Holden, who for seventy-two years, 1772–1844, was minister of the chapel, probably a record in dissenting ministries.

Vita Selectorum Aliquot Virorum (1681), by William Bates, was the gift "Vigil of S. Andrew A.D. 1845" of Edmund Halifax Hansell (1814–1884), Anglican scholar and divine, to "John Rouse Bloxham" (1807–1891), historian of Magdalen College and one time curate to John Henry Newman.

Conyers Middleton's *Free Inquiry into the Miraculous Powers of the Church* (1749) is signed by "Robert Scott," said to have been "bought in Milton," and purchased from R. Scott by W. Walker, October 10, 1793. Six years later it was the property of Lant Carpenter whilst a student at Glasgow, and was presented to the Library by his son, Russell Lant Carpenter.

Novum Testamentum Graecum E Codice MS. Alexandrino (1786), a folio previously owned by Dr. John Disney, contains an inscription: " Frederick Sharpe, Highbury Place, the gift of his father 1855 Nov. 12." It was presented to the Library by Miss Emily Sharpe.

Two biblical scholars, contemporaries, whose works are in the Library, are represented by two presentation copies. Kennicott's *Dissertation* (1753) is stated to be "Don. Auth. April 26, 1755," and Lardner's Sermons (1735–1744), bound in one volume, are inscribed "E. Ch. Blackmore Don. Authoris." Edward Chewning Blackmore had been educated for the ministry at Findern Academy and at Glasgow College. He was the descendant of an ejected minister and a friend of Lardner, Cardale, and other liberal dissenting divines.

Kennicott's great work, *Vetus Testamentum Hebraicum* (two volumes folio, 1776), contains the bookplate of John Kentish

(1768–1853), from whom it passed to Samuel Bache (1804–1876), and, as a plate indicates, was "presented by his family to the College in 1904."

A copy of the Hebrew Bible (1705) contains six inscriptions in Latin of German owners in 1708, 1761, 1762, and 1793, one of the gift by an uncle to the recipient. MS. notes are added by Philemon Moore, from whose library the book came to the College.

Reflections upon Liberty and Necessity, published anonymously in 1761 without name of publisher, contains a MS. note addressed to "Dr. Dawson," giving a list of corrections to be made in the text, adding: "I hope Dr. Dawson will not think this edition quite so execrable as the last, I am sure he will be so candid as to consider it as only wrote for the amusement of a few friends, and not designed for the publick, and likewise to forgive the impropriety of its being put into his hands." The first edition was published in 1759. The volume is not one we should read "for amusement," but the friends of the author may have had other notions of light reading. That the book is rare is plain from the author's statement in the preface: "No copy shall, with my consent, be sold." He is said to have been William Cory, a man of property, who shot himself August 3, 1763.

Harmer's *Observations on Scripture* (four volumes, 1808) was "Presented by the Trustees of Manchester College, York, to Mr. John Colston as a Prize for the best delivered Oration at the examinations 1832. William Turner, Visitor."

William Turner (1761–1859) was a friend and correspondent of Lindsey and Priestley, and contributed a series of valuable historical articles to the *Monthly Repository* under the signature of V. F. (Vigilius Filius), Vigilius having been one of the signatures of his father in Priestley's *Theological Repository.*

One of several editions of Towgood's *Dissenting Gentleman's Three Letters* (1918) was "the gift of Dr. William Bruce, Belfast, 1830, to William Turner," and thus two eminent Unitarian scholars—Irish and English—are associated with a work by an Arian divine, "which," says the Rev. J. H. Colligan, the Presbyterian historian, "for three generations remained the standard work on Dissent, and has been more frequently reprinted, both in England and America, than any other publication of the kind." Amongst the volumes presented by William Turner himself to friends is one of his *Sermons and Addresses,* containing the bookplate of Henry Turner, and remarkable for the bold signature "William Turner, Sept. 20, 1854, aged 93." The writer already named, who was the minister in Mrs. Gaskell's *Ruth*, died in Manchester, April 24, 1859. A student of Warrington Academy and its first historian, he lived to see the foundation of the Unitarian College in 1854.

Job Orton's *Exposition of the Old Testament*, with the Life of the Author by Andrew Kippis (six volumes, 1882), beautifully bound, was "presented to the Library at High Street Chapel, Shrewsbury, by Mr. James Webster, Parish Clerk of St. Chad's Church, 1869." A manuscript note in another hand runs: "This Exposition was drawn up by Mr. Orton for the pulpit, and delivered by him at Shrewsbury in the former part of the Morning Service during a period of more than 21 years, being commenced 16th June, 1744, and the last one on his Birthday, 15th Sept. 1765." Job Orton, formerly minister at High Street Chapel, was buried in St. Chad's Church where there is a memorial to his memory.

James Yates' *Vindication of Unitarianism* (1815) was presented "To the Rev. Dr. Carpenter from the Glasgow Unitarian Fund as a small testimony of the gratitude of its members for his many and important services to the cause of Truth." It is signed "George Harris, Secretary," and dated "April 7th, 1815." The controversy between James Yates M.A., F.R.S., the first President of the College, and Dr. Ralph Wardlaw, the Congregational divine, of which this volume formed part, was destined to be of little consequence compared with that George Harris himself aroused ten years later, which led to litigation lasting twelve years, costing £10,000, and resulting in the loss by Unitarians of the administration of the valuable Lady Hewley Charity.

In the first of two volumes on the celebrated Liverpool Controversy of 1839 is printed a note, expressing the sentiments of the three congregations in the city, beginning: "These volumes together with a Purse containing One Hundred and Fifty Pounds are respectfully presented to the Reverend James Martineau in grateful acknowledgment of the service therein rendered by him to the Cause of Religious Truth."

John Ashworth's *Letters on the Rise of Unitarian Doctrine at Rochdale* . . . (1817) was the gift of Dr. John Thomson (1782–1818), who had first introduced the Methodist Unitarians to the general Unitarian public, was responsible for the book being written, and saw it through the press. It is dated "Leeds,

29 Jany. 1818." The book was published August, 1817. In Northgate End Chapel, Halifax, is a monument to the memory of Thomson by Chantrey, the famous sculptor.

William Gaskell's *Sermon on the Death of John Ashton Nicholls,* With a Sketch of his Life (1859) was presented " to J. B. Smith M.P. with the kind regards of Mr. Nicholls." J. A. Nicholls was the first lay-secretary of the College, to whose memory the Nicholls Hospital in Hyde Road was erected by his father, a stained glass window placed in Longsight Free Christian Church by his mother, a tablet placed in Cross Street Chapel by the congregation, and a memorial erected in Ancoats by public subscription. J. B. Smith was chairman of the Anti-Corn Law League and father of Lady Durning-Lawrence, who with her sisters endowed in his memory the English Chair at Owens College.

The first volume of *Academical Lectures on the Jewish Scriptures and Antiquities* by John Gorham Palfrey (four volumes, 1838–1852) is inscribed " To his Reverence Lant Carpenter LLD. With the Author's affectionate regards. Cambridge Mass. 18 Jan. 1838." The recipient's son, Russell Lant Carpenter, adds: " Revd. Dr. Palfrey was minister of the Church in Brattle Square, Boston, from 1818 to 1830. . . . Ultimately, he resigned his professorship at Harvard, and engaged in politics on the Free Soil (Anti-Slavery) side. His father, a Boston merchant, settled in New Orleans, and left slaves by his Will. Dr. Palfrey set free those who fell to his share."

Two volumes of his own *Speeches, Addresses and Occasional Sermons* were presented " To the Hon. Edward Twistledon with the New Year Wishes of Theodore Parker, Jany. 1, 1851," the great Anti-Slavery advocate.

The catalogue of the Manchester Free Library Reference Department was presented by the City Library Committee to Dr. J. R. Beard, first Principal of the College, in 1864 as an acknowledgment of his revision of it. The second volume, comprising additions from 1864 to 1879, was presented to the Library, with other volumes, by the Manchester Reform Club.

Alexander Gordon's prizes, won whilst a student at Edinburgh University (1856–1859), inscribed by the professors who awarded them, include *The Lyrical Dramas of Aeschylus Translated into English Verse,* by John Stuart Blackie (two volumes, 1850), with the author's inscription in Greek commemorating Gordon's success.

The *Catalogue of the Library at Bamburgh Castle in the County of Northumberland* (two volumes, 1859) were presented to Alexander Gordon by Henry Crosskey D.Sc. (1826–1893) on September 9, three weeks before his death. Gordon noted the date of his death on the letter from the donor included in the volume. Crosskey says of the Library: " It seems very rich in curious pamphlets, illustrative of the religious history of England, and I thought, therefore, might have a special value for you in your favourite studies. . . . It was given me, when I visited the Castle, by a courteous Canon in charge of the Library, and he expressed a strong desire to make its contents useful to any student."

Extracts from the Diary of the Rev. Robert Meeke (1658–1724), edited by Henry James Morehouse F.S.A. With a Brief Sketch of his life, was presented to the " Rev. William Blazeby B.A., with the Editor's kind regards." Published by subscription, it contains an interesting entry by the Diarist, incumbent of Slaithwaite Church for nearly forty years under date November 23, 1689: " About 2 o'clock I went with a friend to Stoney bank, near Holmfirth, and lay all night there, found an old acquaintance who was come to preach at Lydgate, a place licensed for private meetings; he and I lay together, blessed be God." Morehouse, whose bequest to the Library has been noted, adds a footnote: " This was at the house of George Morehouse of Stoney bank, the editor's ancestor, where he was not an infrequent, and always without doubt, a welcome guest. After the lapse of nearly two hundred years, it is gratifying to the editor to discover an intimate friendship between these good men. . . . George Morehouse had been brought up with a decided attachment to the Established Church, and the change which took place in his views was not made without a painful struggle, and involved great sacrifices. . . . He was led to associate himself with those religious teachers with whose efforts for resisting the encroachments of the most dogmatic and intolerant of all churches, he cordially sympathised."

Shakespeare and The Emblem Writers, by Henry Green M.A. (1870), is inscribed " The Rev. William Binns with the author's kind regards. Henry Green. Knutsford. Dec. 7, 1869." It is the gift of one of the first visitors of the College to one of its first, and ablest, students, and as the preface is dated August 10, 1869, and 1870 is the date of publication, must have been one of the first copies from the press.

The two volumes of Martineau's *Hours of Thought* (1876,

1879) were presented by him to his youngest daughter, and are inscribed "Edith Martineau, with J.M.'s love," and the first volume is dated "Nov. 1, 1876."

The History of the Primitive Methodist Connexion, by J. Petty and J. Macpherson (1886), was presented, April 22, 1893, to a leading Methodist on laying a memorial stone of a Primitive Methodist Church in Manchester. It came to the Library from Ireland. Why it travelled from Manchester there is an unsolved problem.

Progress and Poverty, by Henry George (Author's Edition, S. Francisco, 1879), of which only 500 copies were printed, was presented to Harold Rylett, an old student of the College, by James G. Maguire, a leading lawyer in S. Francisco and a personal friend of the author.

Unpublished Letters from Samuel Taylor Coleridge to the Rev. John Prior Estlin, communicated by Henry A. Bright, one-time President of the College, to the Philobiblion Society (1884), was presented to "George Shaw Lefevre" by the editor in the year of publication.

The Booklover's Enchiridion (4th ed., 1884), by Alexander Ireland, was presented by him "to his old friend R. Smiles, Dec. 16, 1886," formerly Manchester City librarian, and, in memory of the latter, to Mr. D. A. Little, "May 28, 1890." Mr. Little was for many years a member of the College Committee, and this book, with others, was presented to the Library by his widow.

James Bonwick (1817–1906), a voluminous writer and an authority on Australian history, presented his *Egyptian Belief and Modern Thought* (1879) to George St. Clair (1836–1908), Unitarian minister, in exchange for the latter's *Buried Cities in Palestine* (1887). Bonwick introduced his book in the letter of presentation with the quaint remark: "I have found an Egyptian book, ready tied for transmission somewhere, and gladly pass it on to you."

Divination and Demonology (1889) by Professor T. Witton Davies, the author's thesis for the degree of Ph.D. at Leipsic in 1887, was presented, March 2, 1899, to the Rev. E. E. Coleman, a Unitarian minister. Davies's *Life of Heinrich Ewald* (1903), his former teacher, was given to Dr. Emrys Jones, of Manchester, with a greeting in Welsh. Dr. Emrys Jones was for many years Honorary Oculist to the College.

Textes Elamite-Semitiques (including the Code of Hammurabi) par V. Scheil O.P. Paris, 1902, is inscribed "The Rev. Charles Hargrove from his friend James Kitson, July, 1903." The donor was the first Lord Airedale, a member of Hargrove's congregation in Leeds. It is not without interest that the editor of the book was a Dominican, the order to which Hargrove belonged before entering (1876) on his thirty-six years' ministry in Leeds.

Worship Song, with Tunes (1905), by W. Garrett Horder, was sent, September 30, 1907, to F. L. Hosmer, one of the most prominent members of what has been called "The Harvard School of Hymnody." In the letter enclosed, Garrett Horder says:

> "Your hymns are great favourites in my church and many others, and at last they are receiving the recognition in this country they deserve. I hope I have had a little part in bringing this about. . . . We are all indebted to you and Mr. Gannett for your beautiful verse. . . ."

The book contains a few notes by Hosmer on the corrections of his hymns by Horder.

Several of the volumes of *The Arden Shakespeare* were edited by Mr. C. Knox Poole, who presented copies to the Rev. J. H. Bibby. In the volume on the *Sonnets* is enclosed a letter dated "14 Ap. 1918" in which the editor observes:

> "I read all the guesses that have been written on "the story of the Sonnets," spent years on it, and decided that no conclusion could be reached for want of evidence. My own impressions are given at the end of the preface, but they are what I call them, impressions, and not conclusions. The edition, though by no means written *virginibus puerisque* is yet too respectable to deal with such work as the late Samuel Butler's, and personally I felt no inclination to rake in mud, or rather, to tell the public about it. . . . I wrote more than eighty pages of introduction, but the publishers hesitated in war-time to print so much, and hinted that less would do, so I cut remorselessly. . . ."

Three tracts by John Taylor, of Norwich (1742, 1751) were the property of John Wiche, General Baptist minister of Maidstone in 1781, then of James Esdaile, Glasgow College, February 14, 1801, who presented the book to the Rev. John Scott Porter, from whose library it was bought by Alexander Gordon in 1880.

Hastings's *Dictionary of the Bible* (five volumes) was presented, March 15, 1910, to the Rev. Thomas Paxton by Sunday School teachers "attending the University Extension Lectures 1909–10 at Birmingham" which he had promoted. The illuminated inscription shows that the teachers were drawn from all denominations, representing the Birmingham Sunday School Union, Birmingham Diocesan Sunday School Institute, the Wesleyan Methodist Sunday School Committee, the Friends' Sunday School Union, and the Midland Sunday School Association.

Friedlander's *Jewish Sources of the Sermon on the Mount* (1911) was given by the author "with kindest remembrances Dec. 11, 1911" to the Rev. E. E. Coleman, and *A Life of Anander Mohan Bose* (1847–1905), the well-known Indian Reformer, by Hem Chandra Sarker, editor of the *Indian Messenger,* was given by him to Mr. Ion Pritchard, a prominent Unitarian.

Books bequeathed by William Blazeby to the College include many given to him: college prizes, gifts from his congregation, etc. One volume, Sir Thomas Browne's *Works* (1831) came to him from Dr. Martineau's library and bears a second inscription: "Miss H. Martineau from her faithful friend T.M.F. 1st Jany. 1836." Another volume originally belonging to Harriet Martineau is a copy of her own *History of the Peace* (four volumes, 1865), published in Boston, U.S.A., of which it is said: "Only seventy-five copies in large paper were printed. It was presented 'To the author with the respects of the publisher.'"

Records of the Family of Heape, by Charles Heape and Richard Heape, of Rochdale (privately printed), 1905, was the gift of Richard Heape, a member of a distinguished Rochdale Unitarian family. It traces the family from 1170 to 1904. A quarto volume, embellished with numerous illustrations, maps, and genealogies, it cost £1,700 to produce.

Cromwell Soldier's Catechism. Facsimiled from one of the only two rare copies formerly known to exist, by Walter Begley, 1900, was given by the editor to Alexander Gordon, who notes: "There are now three copies, two being in the possession of W. Begley (1903)."

Thirty-five volumes of the *Proceedings* of the Liverpool Literary and Philosophical Society (1841–1894) were "presented to the Library of the Unitarian Institute, Liverpool, by Miss

H. E. Higginson in 1890." The donor expressed a wish that "in case this Library should at any time be dispersed the volumes should find a place in one of the libraries connected with our chapels, or in some other not less public library." On the dissolution of the Institute, they were transferred to Hope Street Chapel Library, whence they came to Summerville, where as many volumes of the *Proceedings* of the Manchester Literary and Philosophical Society from its foundation had already found a home. The *Proceedings* of the Liverpool Society include some of the earliest historical work of Alexander Gordon.

Morley's *Life of Gladstone* (three volumes, 1905), beautifully bound, was "presented to Christopher James Street M.A., LL.B., together with an illuminated address and a range of bookshelves by the Bolton Temperance Union on the occasion of his leaving Bolton, Oct. 18, 1908," and with many other works were bequeathed to the College by the recipient.

Thomas Andrews, Shipbuilder, by Shan F. Bullock (1912), was "presented to Mr. and Mrs. C. J. Street, 9 Oct., 1912, by John M. Andrews," brother of the shipbuilder, who went down with the *Titanic* on April 14 that year. The donor, a member of a well-known Unitarian family, is in the Northern Ireland Cabinet.

Early Stages of the Quaker Movement in Lancashire, by Benjamin Nightingale (1921) was presented to Norman Penney, the Quaker scholar, by the author, and contains Penney's corrections of the text.

In 1925, through the good offices of Dr. L. W. Grensted, formerly Principal of Egerton Hall, Manchester, a few Unitarian books, presented to University College, Oxford, by Professor Goldwin Smith, were given to the Library. Each book bears the University College coat of arms, and the following printed inscription: "E Libris in Bibliotheca Collegii Universitatis apud Oxonienses servatis, quos Goldwino Smith, Ejusdem Collegii Socio D.D. Cives Reipublicae Americanae A.S. MDCCCLXIV." Goldwin Smith (1823–1910), scholar and controversialist, was from 1858–1866 Regius Professor of Modern History at Oxford. He visited the States in 1864 and met many Unitarians. From 1868–1872 he was Professor of History at Cornell University, U.S.A., and later settled at Toronto. His gift of Unitarian books to University College, Oxford, was doubtless intended to work as a leaven in the mass of orthodox opinion there. In theology, as in politics, he was a radical.

A number of books, early and late, betray the profound human interest attaching to books in a library.

A copy of Beza's edition of the New Testament (1611) was given by a lover to his lass. The words that are scribbled at the end of the book hardly conceal even now the heartache of the gallant penman. "Good sweet Magee. I desire you to love me that am yr most humble Servant to defend yr beauty, T. Williams."

In Richard Baxter's *Treatise on Self Denial* (1675) we read: "Mrs. Ann Eskricke Her Book, Given Her by Her Mother." Doubtless the mother had in mind the nature of the treatise, and the daughter fondly recalled, after the decease of the donor, the affection that prompted the gift.

An edition of *Poetae Minores Graeci* (1671) takes us back to "the whining schoolboy with his satchel and shining morning face, creeping, like snail, unwillingly to school." Its inscription runs: "E libris Thomi Eglinton. Ex dono Johannis Hoo-Armigeri, June 6, 1741." Then comes the pupil's attempt to write his own name in Greek letters. At the foot, he adds: "My Lesson is in 423." The next page has three verses of a sort, badly written, beginning "For those groves with content and tranquility," expressing the writer's linging to "where they hear not the voice of the taskmaster."

Francis Hutcheson's *Essay on the Nature and Conduct of the Passions and Affections* (published anonymously in 1728) is signed in a fair round hand: "Katharine Blount, Given me by Mrs. A. C." Did a matron hope she was giving her young friend something that should be of service to her in the delicate affairs of the heart? It may be so, though the title "Mrs." was then given to both married and unmarried women.

Our Lord's Prayer in One Hundred Different Languages, "Published for the Benefit of the Poor Cretan Refugees now in Greece," is a memorial of the sufferings of Cretan Christians at the hands of the Turks, 1864–1868. It was "Presented to the Library by Mr. William Thornber, of Sale, through John R. Beard, Dec. 27, 1869."

Bagster's *Comprehensive Bible* was presented to a Welsh Dissenting minister "as a tribute of affection and gratitude for past kindness by an old pupil." Names and dates are given. Between the Testaments is a family register. The last entry is that of the death of a promising young man, an only son, educated for the ministry, a grandson of the minister to whom the book was presented. His military career from September, 1914, is given, and a short account of his death after the Armistice at the hands of an Arab rebel. This is not the only trace of the tragedy of the Great War in the Library. *Pictures from France* (1919), a series of sketches by an *alumnus* of the College, is inscribed by his widow, " In Remembrance of Student Days." Another volume, autographed by its former owner, was presented by his parents to Willaston School as a memorial of an old pupil, who was a Captain and awarded a posthumous V.C. before he was 20; and one shelf is almost full of handsomely bound volumes, which, being opened, reveal the fact that they were prizes won at a great public school by a brilliant classical scholar, afterwards a University lecturer, who also lost his life during those dark days. *Luther and the Reformation* (1914), by Leonard D. Agate M.A., was presented " To the Library of the Unitarian Home Missionary College with the author's compliments 25 II, 14." The author, a graduate in history of Manchester and Cambridge, was the only son of the Rev. Dendy Agate B.A., Honorary Secretary of the College, 1887–1903, and served it as assistant tutor for one year, 1910–1911. Subsequently, he was ordained and, at the end of the war, joined the Church Army at Cologne, where he contracted influenza, from which he died, May 8, 1920, on his return home. Most of his books and those of his father were given later to the College. *The History of the 2/3rd East Lancashire Field Ambulance* (1930), presented by an old student of the College, incidentally relates how he was " awarded the Military Cross for gallantry."

One volume may be said to be a pathetic reminder of the tragedy of the peace. It is a Life of Masaryk, the first President of the Czechoslovak Republic, published in 1930, and presented to the Library, July 2 of that year, by a Czech student of the College. Its last words, reporting Masaryk's address to school-children at Prague in 1928, are: " We are all equal, we must all be free. . . . Perhaps in this company there stands a future President of the Republic. . . . In thirty or forty years you will be speaking to the children from this place. . . . You must carry out our high ideals, the ideals of our history." Ten years later came the Munich agreement, followed on March 15, 1939, by the downfall of the Republic. But the end is not yet.

G

VI—Nonconformist Academies

HE Library constitutes a link between the College and its predecessors, the Nonconformist Academies, in the seventeenth and eighteenth centuries. The fare offered at these early schools of the prophets may be sampled not only in published works but also in lectures and students' notes in manuscript. Two volumes afford first-hand evidence of the character and work of Richard Frankland (1630–1698), the ejected minister, founder of the Academy at Rathmell in 1670. Both were written by James Clegg (1679–1753), one of his pupils, namely, *Discourse on the Death of John Ashe* (a fellow student), 1736, and *The Diary and Autobiography* of James Clegg, edited by Henry Kirke and published in 1899. The former is a very scarce volume. The writings of several pupils of Frankland also illustrate the training they received. One volume relates to a pupil who entered the Academy in its first year. *The Sermons of Thomas Whitaker A.M.*, edited by Thomas Bradbury, was published in 1712. Two other pupils of Frankland contributed to it; Timothy Jollie, then head of the Academy at Attercliffe, writing a Memoir of Whitaker, and Thomas Dickenson adding two sermons preached on the occasion of his death. Of Whitaker's own sermons, one is on the death of Jeremiah Gill, a pupil first of Frankland and afterwards of Jollie. In the preface Bradbury mentions that to the church at Leeds, where he settled in 1675, Whitaker " did the offices of a faithful pastor near 34 years. When he was separated from 'em in the latter end of K. Charles's reign and the beginning of K. James's, it might well be called no more than an absence in body. For the space of 18 months he every week writ out those Sermons that he would have deliver'd in person, had not Satan hinder'd him." The reference is to the preacher's imprisonment for his fidelity to principle in York Castle.

In addition to Bradbury's memorial of this *alumnus* of Rathmell, the Library contains two copies of his MS. sermons, entitled *The Spiritual Marriage, or The Union of Christ to Believers set forth and explained in Twenty-two Sermons, from Jeremiah C. III, 14, by the Revd. and Learned Mr. Thomas Whitaker of Leeds.* One copy was the property of Joseph Ryder (1693–1768), a layman and member of Call Lane Church first under William Moult, a pupil at Attercliffe, who succeeded Thomas Whitaker in 1711 and was minister until his death September 15, 1729, and then under Thomas Whitaker secundus, whose ministry, covering nearly half a century, terminated in 1776, two years before his death, August 4, 1778, at the age of eighty. Ryder states that he bought the sermons, October 1, 1723, and the first sermon is said to have been preached " Jan. 10, 1675." The other copy belonged to the Rev. Joseph Marshall, a pupil at Hoxton Academy under David Jennings, minister of Lydgate Chapel (1765–1814), a native of Leeds, whose ancestors for many generations had worshipped at Call Lane Chapel. A manuscript volume of sermons seems to have been compiled by Thomas Whittaker at the request of his congregation shortly before his death, as a memorial for their benefit. The sermons cover 300 8vo pages, and are followed by verses celebrating the pious joy of the preacher on the completion of his labours. In the preface the writer expresses his reluctance to let his sermons " run the gauntlet of a critical and censorious world." It is curious that he should have had his wish, but whether willy or nilly no man can say. Seeing that the sermons were not destined to be published, two disciples of Whittaker apparently obtained the loan of the manuscript and made the two transcripts. Between them the Whittakers, father and son, occupied the one pulpit for eighty-two years— a tenure almost as exceptional as the preaching of twenty-two sermons on one text. It may be added that the Library also possesses the manuscript diary (May 25, 1733–January 2, 1768) of Joseph Ryder in forty-one stoutly bound vellum quarto volumes, presented to the College in 1925 by Edgar Lupton Esq., of Leeds, his collateral descendant.

Of the tutors and pupils of the numerous academies that followed Frankland's, there are many published works in the Library. Some are of peculiar interest on account of the notes they contain.

An early Hebrew Bible printed by Plantin (1580) was the property of three members of a family of Unitarian scholars; two of whose signatures it bears, viz. John Turner (1689–1737)

---

[1] See Art. by the writer in *Transactions of the Unitarian Historical Society.* iv. 248-267.

and William Turner, of Newcastle (1761–1859), pupils respectively at the academies at Manchester and Warrington. Their MS. notes, which crowd the margins of the pages, afford some evidence of Semitic studies in the academies named, and those relating to Manchester as peculiarly valuable in view of the lack of information on the subject.

A Greek Testament, published by Roger Daniel, 1653, was purchased by James Belsham, father of Thomas Belsham, in 1731. It is interleaved, contains notes " ex doctissimis auctoribus collectis," and was formerly in the library of the General Baptist Academy, founded 1694. James Belsham had been a pupil at Stratford-on-Avon under John Fleming, and his dated notes, mostly in Latin with references in Greek, Syriac, and Hebrew, were collected whilst a student.

The academy at Kibworth and Hinckley is represented by *Logica in Usum Juventutis Academicae*, Northampton, 1721, and *Miscellanea in Usum Juventutis Academicae*, Northampton, 1721, both by the tutor, John Jennings, of Philip Doddridge. These books had, of course, a very limited circulation.

A copy of Doddridge's *Lectures* (1768) was used by Lant Carpenter in 1798, when a student at Northampton Academy. This academy, under John Horsey, had been founded by Doddridge in 1729, and from the Latin MS. of his tutor John Jennings he had borrowed the form and some of the substance of his lectures. In his copy of the *Lectures*, Lant Carpenter made copious notes in a neat hand, including excerpts from various theological text-books in vogue among Nonconformist students of the period, brought to his notice by his tutor. Of Doddridge's own published works, most are in the Library.

The immediate successor of Doddridge was Caleb Ashworth (1722–1775), under whom the academy moved to Daventry, where Joseph Priestley was a student. In 1763, Dr. Ashworth published a small *Hebrew Grammar* for the use of his pupils. Published anonymously, it was afterwards a text-book at Hoxton and Rotherham. As early as 1785 (April 13) Thomas Belsham, then tutor at Daventry, reported to the Coward Trustees that the book " was entirely out of print," and the Trustees expressed a wish that he should " provide for the printing of a new edition " at their expense. The wish was not fulfilled, and copies of the book are extremely rare. Alexander Gordon, who wrote the lives of Ashworth and Priestley in the *Dictionary of National Biography*, despite diligent search in libraries throughout the country, had never seen a copy until he saw one in the Library at Summerville many years after he ceased to be Principal of the College. In 1804, however, Thomas Yeates, All Souls, Oxford, who matriculated there in 1802 but never graduated, professed to revise the grammar, with the addition of what is described as " an elegant engraving " and certain " Directions " to students, but without any acknowledgment to Caleb Ashworth. He may not have known the name of the author, though Professor D. S. Margoliouth, in the *Dictionary of National Biography,* says he " was employed by the publishers of Caleb Ashworth's Hebrew Grammar to revise the third and subsequent editions," whatever that may mean precisely. Ashworth's Grammar was published at Cambridge by the University printer, Yeates' was published in London by Jordan and Maxwell. A copy of the so-called " revision " is in the Library, bearing the autograph of William Johns, the intimate friend of John Dalton and one time tutor at the Manchester Academy under Thomas Barnes. An examination of it proves that the revision amounted to little or nothing.

Four volumes of MS. notes of lectures delivered at Daventry Academy by Thomas Belsham, 1786–1788, on Moral Philosophy and Divinity were written by Thomas W. Paterson (d. 1812), who succeeded his tutor in the ministry at Daventry, and was afterwards at Ashby de la Zouche and Bardon. His son, Alexander Paterson M.A. (1799–1852), was minister at Stourbridge and Cradley.

A reprint of the Savoy *Declaration of the Faith and Order . . . in the Congregational Churches* bears the signature of " W. Parry " (1754–1819), tutor at Wymondley, where the academy moved in 1799 from Northampton, and of his colleague " Joseph Turnbull," dated " 1823," together with a few manuscript notes.

Eight volumes of notes taken down from 1763 to 1769 at Hoxton Academy introduces us to the orations of Andrew Kippis and John Eames. As the last-named tutor died in 1744, and published nothing, it is clear that these notes were taken down from Abraham Rees, the Arian tutor in mathematics. Three volumes are in Latin, two in shorthand, and only two in English. The subjects are Natural Philosophy, Belles Lettres, Chronology, and the History of Eloquence and Oratory, the latter containing all " Quotations in the original language." The penman was William Wood, who afterwards succeeded Joseph Priestley at Mill Hill Chapel, Leeds.

From Homerton Academy is a volume of MS. lectures by John Conder D.D. on Christian Theology, delivered before 1781, and taken down by Richard Fry (1759-1845), who was first a Congregational minister and then Unitarian minister at the New Meeting, Kidderminster, 1813-1836.

Warrington Academy is well represented by both manuscript and printed works. A bound volume of papers and MS. letters from 1754-1768 covers the whole period of its inception, life, and end. It includes prospectuses, reports, and letters written by officers, tutors and prominent supporters. Collected by Samuel Heywood (1753-1828), pupil at Warrington, 1768-1772, it was presented (1854) by Sir Benjamin Heywood (1795-1865) to Henry Arthur Bright (1830-1884), historian of the academy and grand-nephew of Samuel Heywood. It includes also MS. letters of Mr. J. M. Thompson, Magdalen College, Oxford, addressed to Alexander Gordon relating to Warrington tutors. A large folio contains a copy of the most important minutes of Warrington Trustees copied (December, 1886) by Francis Nicholson from the original in two volumes at Manchester College, Oxford.

Amongst the printed works by tutors of the academy is the rare *Course on the Theory of Language and Universal Grammar*, by Joseph Priestley, printed by William Eyres in 1762. It was afterwards used as a text-book at Hoxton by Andrew Kippis. Hebrew and Greek characters were not printed in the text, but spaces were left for them to be inserted in writing. Another work by Priestley, *The Rudiments of English Grammar* (1769), as a note informs us, " passed through several editions." This edition was printed during Priestley's residence in Leeds. J. T. Rutt, the editor of Priestley's works, states that he had never been able to see a copy with the frontispiece by Fuseli, although search had been made in the British Museum.

Two folio volumes of the *Hebrew Concordance*, by John Taylor, the first principal tutor at Warrington, were bequeathed by his grandson, the Rev. Philip Taylor, of Dublin, to Dr. Martineau, who began his ministry as Philip Taylor's assistant. They were presented by Miss Martineau to the Hebrew prizeman at Manchester College in the year of Dr. Martineau's death, and given by him to the Library. In his address at the Centenary Soiree of Manchester College, held in London, June 23, 1886, Dr. Martineau referred to this work. Speaking of the Warrington Academy, he said: " Some of the most delightful friendships of my early settled life were with a few of the *alumni* of the Warrington Academy. Some visible relics of those times I still reverently preserve, gifts or bequests of Mr. Philip Taylor; one, a copy of Dr. John Taylor's *Hebrew Concordance,* which was the author's personal possession." Another book written by John Taylor and formerly owned by him, is *A Paraphrase with Notes on the Epistle to the Romans* (1752). Amongst numerous notes in it is the following: " Quae in hoc libro manu scribuntur, praesertim ad paginas 364 et 365 ab auctore esse scripta, ipse auctor, nomine subscripto, testor. Johann. Taylor."

A rare volume in a controversy on Liturgies or Free Prayers in which John Taylor and John Seddon, of Warrington Academy, took opposite sides, is *Remarks . . . concerning the Expediency of Forms of Prayer,* published anonymously by John Brekell in 1762. H. D. Roberts, in his History of Hope Street Church, Liverpool, said there was no copy in the British Museum, Dr. Williams' library, nor in any Liverpool library, though he afterwards found one in the John Rylands Library, Manchester. The unfortunate controversy materially assisted in retarding the progress of the academy.

The works of Gilbert Wakefield, professor at Warrington, 1779–1783, include his fine edition of Lucretius (three volumes, quarto, 1796). " The first edition," says his biographer, " is somewhat rare in consequence of the destruction of many copies by a fire at the printer's warehouse."

In 1790, Wakefield became classical tutor at the Hackney College, but resigned in the following year. Of this ill-fated college there is an ample memorial in a volume of sermons and tracts relating to its rise and fall, in addition to copies of works by the members of its staff, and a MS. volume of lectures delivered there. The last mentioned is a course of twenty lectures on " The Existence and Attributes of God," by Thomas Belsham, taken down in 1790 by Charles Well-beloved, who added a table of contents. Each lecture is followed by a reference to books prescribed by the tutor. It is interesting to observe that Priestley printed his *Heads of Lectures in a Course of Experimental Philosophy . . .* delivered at the New College in Hackney (1794), as he tells us in the preface, " to save the students the trouble of transcribing them."

John Mill's *Novum Testamentum* (folio, 1707) affords evidence of the painstaking diligence of another tutor at Hackney. John Pope, an old student of Exeter under Samuel

Merivale and Micaijah Towgood, was tutor in classics 1791–1793. He numbered the paragraphs of the double-columned Latin Prolegomena of 168 pages, greatly enlarged the index, and on its wide margin wrote countless notes in Greek and shorthand. The first note, which he signed, provides an indication of the time and labour spent on the work. " In the gospel of Matthew, I have copied exactly R. Stephen's margin from his edition of the New Testament of 1550. For the rest, I have only corrected the margin of Mill in his transcript from this edition, so that this may be regarded as corresponding exactly to Stephen's copy. A list of Stephen's errors is at the end of the volume."

To John Pope also we owe information respecting Samuel Jones (1680–1719), an eminent tutor at Gloucester and Tewkesbury, 1708–1720, whose pupils included Joseph Butler and Thomas Secker. In the preface to *The Works of Thomas Secker* (six volumes, 3rd ed., 1775), formerly owned by Pope, the life of the Archbishop is sketched by Bp. Porteus, and reference made to his education " in the academy of one Mr. Jones at Gloucester and Tewkesbury." Nothing is said of his earlier studies at Attercliffe under Timothy Jollie, or of his preaching in Nonconformist chapels. In a marginal note, Pope wrote at some length eulogising the scholarship and ability of Samuel Jones, and corrects the text where Secker's abandonment of Nonconformity is mentioned. This he attributes, not, with Porteus, to his " more extensive judgment, reading and knowledge," but to his " views of interest and loss of principle." Which opinion of Secker's motive in conforming is correct cannot be determined, but the tribute to Samuel Jones by John Pope is that of one scholar and tutor to another.

The academies at Exeter are represented by a number of books formerly in the libraries of those eighteenth century training schools. *The Memoirs of the Life, Character, and Writings of Philip Doddridge*, by Job Orton (1767), contains an inscription by Doddridge's former pupil and assistant at Northampton: " The gift of the Author to the General Academy at Exon." The first academy at Exeter had been kept by Joseph Hallett (1656–1722), who was assisted by his son of the same name (1691–1744), whose valuable *Free and Impartial Study of the New Testament* (three volumes, 1729–1736) is in the Library.

The second academy under Samuel Merivale, Micaijah Towgood, and John Turner began in 1760, and the library belonging to Taunton Academy (1670–1759) was removed to Exeter. One book, Sale's *Translation of the Koran* (1st ed., quarto, 1734) bears an inscription showing that it was originally at Taunton. The third Exeter Academy under Timothy Kenrick and Joseph Bretland (1799–1805) had the use of the library in the second academy. These books have in fact been in the libraries in turn of Taunton, second Exeter, Hackney College, third Exeter, and Manchester College, York. They returned to Manchester with the last-named college, went to London with it, and now are at Manchester College, Oxford. The volumes at Summerville made a further journey to Manchester amongst duplicate acquired in 1874 from the College.

Manchester College is represented by the published works of its tutors from its foundation, in 1786, by Thomas Barnes, Minister of Cross Street Chapel, Manchester. A volume of MS. lectures on "Universal Grammar," by Ralph Harrison (1748–1810), tutor in Manchester College, dated 1787–1788, are in shorthand. They are largely based on Priestley's lectures at Warrington, where Harrison was a pupil, and are illustrated by quotations. The Greek is without accents or breathings, but the Hebrew is pointed. A portion of Harrison's MS. diary is also in the Library. Ralph Harrison's MS. remains are the more important because his colleague, Thomas Barnes D.D., in his will left strict instructions that all his own steno-graphic MSS. and diaries should be burnt unread. Many volumes in the Library formerly owned by Manchester College tutors contain their notes.

The first Manchester Academy (1690–1713) is brought before us by a transcript of the funeral sermon by John Chorlton, its tutor, on the death of his colleague, Henry Newcome (1695), his colleague in the ministry, whose published sermons (1660) were presented to the Library by one of his successors in the ministry and tutor at the College, J. G. Robberds.[1]

Rerum Anglicarum Scriptores Post Bedam (folio, 1596), edited by Sir Henry Savile, contains two bookplates of William Boynton Strickland and Eustace Strickland, two members of a well-known Yorkshire family, and the signature of " C. Well-beloved, York, 1840," followed by the letters E.A.C.A.A.C.M.E., which, being interpreted, mean " Ex aere collato ab alumnis Collegii Mancuniensis Ebor." It is one of several volumes purchased from the fund presented to Wellbeloved in his retirement from the college at York, of which he was Principal from 1803 to 1840.

---

[1] See also p. 18.

Several volumes of MS. lectures by J. G. Robberds, Professor of Hebrew and Syriac at Manchester College, 1840–1845, and of Pastoral Theology, 1840–1852, constituted one of the earliest donations to the Library. Many volumes of lecture notes, taken down from Martineau, Tayler, Bowman, and Finlay by William Blazeby when a student at Manchester College, formed part of his bequest to the Library. Another set of notes taken down (1860) by Alexander Gordon from Tayler and Martineau are also here. Two volumes of pamphlets by James Martineau include letters and tracts printed for private circulation only, a folio contains press notices of his speeches and addresses from 1838 to 1895, and eight 12mo volumes contain his lectures on the New Testament given to a class during his ministry in Liverpool, 1840–1845.

The marble medallion of John James Tayler, professor 1840–1857, principal 1853–1869, formerly in Upper Brook Street Church, Manchester, of which he was the first minister, was presented by the trustees of the chapel, and placed in the new Library building. More recently, the Library acquired by gift the invitation to Tayler to become minister of Mosley Street Chapel (1820), signed by all the members, and the address, also signed by the members, presented to him in 1853 on leaving Upper Brook Street Chapel, together with a similar address on the same occasion from the Lower Mosley Street Schools, and his own bound volumes of his collected printed lectures, sermons, etc. A bound volume of notes of lectures on Galatians and Romans by Dr. James Drummond, professor 1869–1885, principal 1885–1906, dated 1876–1877, was formerly in the library of C. J. Street M.A., LL.B., a former pupil of Manchester College. Books from the library of Dr. Drummond contain valuable critical notes. He appears to have been the first of many tutors writing in shorthand to employ the Pitman system. Twenty-six volumes were originally " granted to Joseph Estlin Carpenter M.A., by the Hibbert Trustees, December 3, 1869 "—the distinguished scholar, who was professor 1875–1906, and principal 1906–1915.

In a volume of the works of S. Ephrem, the Syrian, edited by J. B. Morris (1857) is an interesting letter by W. E. Addis, professor 1900–1910, discussing the editor of the book named and other writers. " Bower knew little of nothing of the sources directly but he lived in the golden age of ecclesiastical criticism and copied freely from French scholars, especially Tillemont. Tillemont's accuracy, as Gibbon says, ' approached genius,' his learning was stupendous, and modern inquiry, which has thrown much light on the origin of Christianity, has added little to our knowledge of the Church in the great patristic age, say from A.D. 200 onwards. Ephrem's Homilies in Morris's translation is a much higher order of work. Morris was a man of real learning, and besides being an accomplished Syriac scholar was deeply read in the Fathers. He was one of the most learned, most innocent, and most eccentric of men. He became a Roman Catholic early in 1846, and his total inability to teach, preach, manage a parish, or keep out of debt led him into endless trouble. He and I were very intimate, and I was with him a few hours before his death. There is a lot of useful learning in his notes on St. Ephraim. Probably I am among the very few who have read a big book of his called *Jesus the Son of Mary*. It abounds in recondite learning buried under extravagances of many kinds. His best work was his translation of Ephrem. . . . "

Archibald Bower (1686–1766) was a Jesuit historian who conformed to the Church of England, was readmitted to the Society of Jesus (1745), but left a second time two years later and was afterwards proved guilty of being secretly a member of the Roman Catholic Church. Tillemont is one of the great seventeenth century historians (sixteen folio volumes, 1701) whose works are in the Library. The note by William Edward Addis (1843–1917) is the more interesting in view of his own singular career. A distinguished scholar of Balliol College, Oxford, who wrote with authority on the Old Testament, he was the son of a Presbyterian minister, joined the Church of Rome in 1866, which he served for twenty-three years, then, after a brief ministry as a free churchman in Melbourne, became in 1893 minister of the High Pavement Chapel, Nottingham, in succession to a line of distinguished Unitarians. Thence he entered Manchester College, Oxford, as tutor in Old Testament, became later a churchman, and in 1910 accepted a living in London where he died.

The Life and Letters of Stopford Brooke (1917) contains a letter by its author, Dr. L. P. Jacks, later principal of Manchester College. An extract will interest the many admirers of the subject of the biography and its author. " What Brooke achieved was considerable, but the interest of his life centres in his personality and not in his work. This, I think, is the mark of true greatness, and corresponds to the right order of values. Christianity preserves that order as its central tenet. I do not and did not feel as you do about Brooke: that he was a larger edition of myself, or of anything within myself. No two men were ever more unlike one another than he and I, and I could only realise his world by an effort of imagination. He was one of the great companions. His emergence in the mid-Victorian times was one of Nature's wildest freaks, for he had next to nothing in common with his environment. A portent—but one that we can love."

Naturally, the staff of the Unitarian College is well represented in the Library. Many of the books formerly owned by Dr. John Relly Beard, principal 1854–1874, are on the shelves, whilst his MS. lectures on Biblical Hermeneutics, a typed and bound biography of him by his son, the late J. R. Beard, and an album containing the portraits of his students, presented to him on his retirement from the principalship, are amongst the memorials of the earliest days of the institution. Amongst the books presented to the Library by the Rev. Henry Green M.A., visitor 1859–1873, are copies of his own works. One—Whitney's *Choice of Emblems,* edited with Notes and Dissertations (1866) —contains the following note: " Of this form of Whitney's *Emblems,* on tone paper, small size, only six copies have been issued. Henry Green, Knutsford, May 15, 1866."

La Syrie, L'Egypte, La Palestine, et Le Judée, by Le Baron Taylor et Louis Reyboud (2t., quarto, Paris, 1839) bears an inscription in Latin which connects the first two tutors of the College, John Relly Beard and William Gaskell, illustrates their friendship, and commemorates a sorrow which befell the senior man. It is dated " Cal. April M.D.C.C.C.L.V.I."

A bound volume contains " Lectures on Preaching and Pastoral Care " in manuscript, by Brooke Herford D.D. (tutor 1860–1875), which were originally given at Harvard University in 1891 and afterwards at Manchester College, Oxford, and (1893) at the Unitarian College, Manchester. They are still as fresh and helpful as when first penned.

A copy of Gebhardt's edition of Tischendorf's *Novum Testamentum* bears the words: " Used by Principal Odgers and later by Alexander Gordon, who twice had it rebound."

The opening lectures, delivered by the Rev. J. E. Manning M.A., whilst tutor of the College, 1894–1910, with his MS. notes and additions, are amongst the number of his books in the Library. Of Alexander Gordon, principal 1890–1911, there are many memorials, including MS. copies of opening

H

lectures (1890–1895), never printed, and a complete collection of his printed sermons and lectures. Of the latter, a few were printed for private circulation only, and it is doubtful if they are to be found elsewhere. Many of his former books in the Library came to him as Hibbert Scholar and Fellow and are inscribed " E Pecuniis Hibbertianis."

Many volumes, chiefly philosophical, previously owned by Edgar Thackray M.A., B.D., Ph.D. (1876–1925), lecturer in Christian Doctrine 1921–1926, together with the typescript of his lectures are in the Library, and a number of books, including some written by him, presented by the Rev. S. H. Mellone M.A., D.Sc., principal of the College 1911–1921.

VII—Manuscripts

IN addition to the numerous manuscripts already noticed,[1] the Library possesses many of peculiar interest to students of Nonconformist and, especially, of Unitarian history.

What has been called " The Primary Document of English Unitarianism " is a Latin manuscript in Lambeth Library, which exhibits in a fraternal spirit the common ground of Islam and Unitarian Christianity. It was originally presented in 1662 by a group of Unitarians to the Ambassador of Morocco, then negotiating with Charles II for the return of Tangiers, which had been ceded to the King as part of the wedding dowry of Catharine of Braganza. Alexander Gordon had the manuscript copied out *verbatim et literatim,* translated large sections of it, and provided the whole with a historical introduction and commentary. It is a thick quarto volume. The "Epistle" prefaced to the manuscript, which Charles Leslie published in 1708, with other attacks upon Unitarians (in an effort to identify Unitarianism with Islam) has been corrected in every detail of spelling, etc., by reference to the original.

Seventeenth and eighteenth century manuscripts include " A Collection of Prayers," dated 1648; " An Examination of Dr. Burnet's Theory of the Earth," by Dr. Keill, dated 1691, seven years before its publication; " Lectures delivered at Edinburgh University by William Leechman " (1706–1783), taken down by a pupil; " Sermons by Caleb Fleming " (two volumes dated 1766–1785); " A Reply to Leland's View of the Principal Deistical Writers," which was published 1734–1736; " Memoirs of the Life and Writings of Daniel Waterland " (1683–1740), by a contemporary; " A Declaration that the Sacrament of the Lord's Supper had been taken by an officer in the Navy, 17 March, 1704," under the Test Act of 1673; " Facsimile of the Ordination Certificate of Cuthbert Harrison B.A., 1651," and

---

[1] See pp. 13, 19, 31, 45, 66, 69, 71, 80, 83, 99, 100, 102, 103, 106, 107, 109.

another of his Absolution by the Bishop of Chester, 1677; Two Facsimiles of Indulgence Licenses, 1672, signed by Arlington, and a third, signed by Clifford; three original Licenses of the dwelling house of John Chubb in Chester, dated 1704, 1711, and 1715, and one of John Williams for the Independents, dated 1760, all taken out under the Toleration Act of 1689, and the original License of William Moon as a preacher, under the Act of 1779. There are letters by Philip Henry, the ejected minister, and others, and A Sermon by Philip Doddridge; also eight letters to Isaac Watts, dated 1727–1740, from various Nonconformist tutors. Three hundred letters addressed to George Benson D.D. (1699–1762) include thirty from Samuel Bourn (1689–1754), eight from Nathaniel Lardner (1694–1752), eight from Caleb Rotheram (1694–1752), seven from Edmund Calamy (1697–1755), eight from William Leechman (1679–1758), and fourteen from other Scottish professors, including Frances Hutcheson, the philosopher. Few, indeed, are the outstanding figures in eighteenth century Nonconformity unrepresented, in addition to Germans like Michaelis and Bomberger, and four letters from Jonathan Mayhew of Boston, U.S.A., the early champion of Unitarianism and political liberty in New England. "An Explication" from Newcome Cappe's Hymn Book (York, 1786) contains manuscript annotations by Charles Wellbeloved.

A thick quarto of 572 pages contains copies of letters written by Philip Doddridge to his friends from 1720–1726. These were transcribed by Thomas Stedman in 1790–1791 from the originals. Most of them were published in *The Diary and Correspondence of Philip Doddridge,* edited by his great-grandson (five volumes, 1829–1831), which are here annotated with notes, but not a few of the printed copies contain corrections and omissions as compared with the manuscript.

The Worthies of Devon, a quarto manuscript written originally by John Fox (1693–1763), is a transcript made by James Northcote, the painter (1746–1831). In an article in the *Christian Life* (April 15, 1899), Alexander Gordon, who had recently acquired the manuscript, gives an account of it and of the transcript in folio by Northcote in the possession of the Plymouth Proprietary Library. From Gordon came also two other volumes relating to John Fox. One contains the printed copy of the Plymouth manuscript, edited by Joshua Brooking Rowe F.S.A. in the *Transactions of the Devonshire Association* 1896–1897, and the other, the autobiography, nine memoirs, and letters of Fox and others, from Fox's original manuscript, afterwards lost, which were printed in *The Monthly Repository*, 1821. The letters, which passed between Fox and Archbishop Secker and Dr. Chandler, are not in the two MS. transcripts by Northcote; there are slight variations between *The Monthly Repository* memoirs and those of both MSS., whilst both these contain memoirs added by Northcote. In this respect the Plymouth MS. is much fuller than the MS. at Summerville, though the latter has one memoir not contained in the former. The quarto manuscript has four engravings, one of which purports to be the picture of Fox, but is really from a portrait of Samuel Richardson, the novelist. In all three volumes in the Library, Alexander Gordon has inserted notes, references, etc., and his correspondence on the subject of the MSS. with J. B. Rowe and J. E. Odgers, together with a collation made by the last named of the Plymouth MS. with the articles in *The Monthly Repository*. In these volumes the Library possesses the most complete and critical account of John Fox, the biographer of Dissenters, from whom, in Gordon's words, "we learn more than from any other sources, respecting the inner life of the West of England and London Dissenters, during the first quarter of the eighteenth century."

Early in 1937 the Rev. W. H. Burgess M.A., of Plymouth, presented to the Library a manuscript history of the General Baptists, Universalists, Free Thinking Christians, and Sabbatarian General Baptists, originally (1907) prepared by him for publication in a larger work on English Nonconformity edited by Dr. J. E. Odgers, which was never completed. It is a careful and scholarly piece of work by one whose competence in this field of study has long been recognised.

In the same year the trustees of Bank Street Chapel, Bury, gave a large typescript history of Bank Street Chapel, 1719–1919, representing many years' research by the Rev. E. D. Priestley Evans. It includes many excerpts from manuscript sources. Shortly before this two typescript lectures by William Hewitson, of Bury, on Local Nonconformity and Some Pioneers and Their Friends, given at Bank Street, Bury, October 20, 1909, February 23, 1910, were presented by the Rev. J. M. Bass M.A., who had used the original manuscript.

A handsomely bound volume contains " Extracts from Letters of the late James Cropper transcribed for his grandchildren by their affectionate mother and aunt, Anne Cropper." A fine engraving of James Cropper is included. James Cropper (1773–1841) was a Liverpool Quaker merchant and philanthropist, and the letters, dating from 1790–1827, include a few from members of his family. Amongst other matters of interest they tell of a tour in Ireland. They are elucidated by *Dingle Bank The Home of the Croppers,* by Frances Anne Conybeare, one of Cropper's descendants, published in 1925. The MS. volume had been in the library of Samuel Fielden, of Todmorden, who was related to the Croppers by marriage.

" A Unitarian Catechism with a View to Religious Instruction for Confirmation " (3rd ed. revised and enlarged, Kolozsvar, 1876), by Joseph Ferencz, is a MS. translated into English by the author, given by Bishop Ferencz to Alexander Gordon in the year named.

Of materials for students of Unitarian history, apart from numerous manuscript notes in printed works, the following may be mentioned: " Papers relating to Bank Street Chapel, Bolton, dating from 1754 "; " Minutes of the Mosley Street Chapel and of Upper Brook Street Church from the foundation of the congregation in 1809 to its dissolution in 1922," together with the records of the graves in both burial yards; " Minutes and Letters relating to the Bolton Missionary Association, 1865–1882 "; " Minutes and Reports of the Missionary Conference from its establishment in 1862 until it was merged in the Ministerial Fellowship in 1930 "; " Lists of Chapels and their Ministers from 1819 to 1881," and the Minutes of " The Brotherhood," a ministerial society meeting in Manchester, 1889–1917.

A collection in three bound volumes of over 300 letters addressed to James Hews Bransby (1763–1847), described by Alexander Gordon in the *D.N.B.* as " a mass of compromising papers which fell into the hands of Franklin Baker, minister of Bank Street Chapel, Bolton, and were probably destroyed." They passed in fact from the minister to his brother, Sir Thomas Baker, and ultimately into the College Library. Of these letters the most interesting and best written are sixteen by two young ladies—sisters and daughters of the manse—who followed the teaching profession. Their delightful effusions, lightly reflecting their joys and sorrows, contain much entertaining gossip respecting men, maids, and manners, strangely contrasting with the sombre musings of ministerial minds seldom unconcerned with theological problems, congregational conflicts, or the brevity and uncertainty of this mortal life.

A large collection of letters written to or by the Rev. and Mrs. Edward Tagart disclose in some detail the character of the life and work of Unitarian ministers and congregations during the first half of the nineteenth century. They also reveal the intimacies of life in cultured circles at Norwich, Manchester, and elsewhere, describe academic and other pursuits in Manchester College, York, and the interests of students outside its walls, and contain *inter alia* a charming yet singularly pathetic love story illustrating the old adage that "the course of true love never did run smooth." Incidentally, an interesting sketch is given of Martineau's first sermon in college by a fellow-student.

The two most illustrious members of the Martineau family, of whose early correspondence this collection contains specimens, are represented also by many epistles of a later period—sixty-eight letters addressed by James Martineau to John and Alexander Gordon, and almost as many of Harriet Martineau to various friends down to 1876. Moreover, in Carpenter's *Life of Martineau* is inserted copies of letters to the author on the subject of the biography, and one from Martineau to Mrs. Lant Carpenter (July 27, 1828) telling of his struggles to express himself in simple language during his first ministry in Dublin. He found it "no easy task for a man to wage war with himself, to imprison his taste, to strangle all his pet thoughts, and to clothe his feelings in the tatters and beggarly elements of colloquial phraseology. . . . "

Of Unitarian ministers of the period 1800–1875, it must suffice to say that there are few of any note whose letters, one or more, are not to be found in the Library. The most valuable for historians of Dissent are those (a considerable number) of Robert Brook Aspland (1805–1869) and Charles Beard (1827–1888), written whilst they were editing the *Christian Reformer* and the *Theological Review* respectively to one or two of their most valued contributors.

In the first volume of the *Letters of Anna Seward* (1747–1809) there is the MS. letter, dated July 17, 1807, from the author addressed to "Mr. A. Constable, Bookseller, Edinburgh." The letter was printed in the "Advertisement" to the volume. Anna Seward, known as "the Swan of Lichfield," moved in the circle of Samuel Johnson. In the letter, she anticipates that her correspondence left to the publisher would run to "Twelve Volumes," though "voluminous as is the collection, it does not include a twelfth part of my epistolary writing from the time it commenced, viz. from the year 1784, to the present day." The letters were actually published in six volumes in 1811.

Other men and women of mark of whose letters there are specimens include Jeremy Bentham, Sir John Bowring, William Cobbett, Sir Humphry Davy, Mrs. Gaskell, Mary Howitt, Washington Irving, Lord Macaulay, Jame Porter, Mary Shelley, and Madam Stael.

Manuscript sermons, bound and unbound, include those of Thomas Belsham, Thomas Sadler, Charles Hargrove, Alexander Gordon, and very many others.

A typescript copy of a manuscript written between 1846 and 1853 gives the Epitaphs and Memorial Inscriptions, 1719–1853, from the graves in the burial ground of the Unitarian Chapel, Bradford, formerly known as the Presbyterian Chapel, Toad Lane, Bradford. When the new chapel was erected in 1869, the gravestones and memorial tablets were dispersed, and only a few survive. The record is the more important since existing registers do not record any burials before 1768. The first interment took place in 1719, the year when the first chapel on the present site was opened. A plan of the old chapel and the burial ground is included, together with full particulars of the Mural Tablets, and an index of names.

The names include those of four ministers, two of whcm, Isaac Wilkinson (1684–1728), "a Pious and Painful Minister of the Gospel," and Robert Richmond (1681–1728), "Minister of the Gospel, late of Clack-Heaton," were not ministers of the chapel, nor of any congregation in the group with which Chapel Lane Chapel afterwards became associated. The parents of Wilkinson, buried in graves on either side of him, were probably members of the congregation. The father, eighty-seven when he died, was born in 1655, and the mother, ninety-four at death, was born in 1648. They were almost certainly amongst the hearers of the earliest ministers of the congregation in the chapel opened in 1688 at Little Horton, near Wibsey, and members of the flock which met in Horton Hall from 1672 to 1688. The ejected Vicar of Bradford, Jonas Water-house (b. 1627), who founded the congregation, was buried in the Parish Church (now Cathedral) in 1716, three years before the opening of Toad Lane Chapel with its burial ground. Two ministers, John Dean (1738–1813) and Nicholas Thomas Heineken (1763–1840) were buried in the chapel where they had ministered for forty-five and twenty-three years respectively. One lengthy inscription to the memory of a doctor of medicine (1763–1824) is in Latin, whilst that of another medical prac-titioner contains a quotation in Greek from Homer's Iliad, which may be rendered: " For a leach is of the worth of many other men for the cutting out of arrows, and the spreading of soothing simples."

A pathetic interest attaches to the laborious work in eight handsomely bound volumes on " The Synoptic Gospels " and " The Book of Proverbs." They were written by Eustace Thompson (1868–1930), an old student of the College, and presented to the Library by his widow, after he had met his death as the result of a motor accident in the North of Ireland.

Two volumes not in manuscript deserve to be mentioned in connection with the Library because of their peculiar appeal to students of the ministry. Their authors are Simon Harwarde (fl. 1572–1614) and John Clarke (d. 1820). Harwarde's life is in the *Dictionary of National Biography.* John Clarke was a schoolmaster at Enfield, where John Keats was a pupil, taught by Charles Cowden Clarke, son of the schoolmaster, whose intimate friend he became. Later, he was a close friend of John Gordon (1807–1880), father of Alexander Gordon, and a few letters of his and of his gifted wife are in the Library.

Harwarde's sermon is one of a collection of sixteenth century sermons, and its title is: " *A Godly and Learned Sermon, Containing a Charge and Instruction for all unlearned and negligent and dissolute Ministers. And an exhortation to the Common People, to seeke their amendment, by Prayer unto God. Preached at Manchester in Lancastershire, before a great and worshipful Audience, by occasion of certaine Parsons there at that present, appointed (as then) to be made Ministers, by Simon Harwarde,* published in 1586.

The title of John Clarke's volume is *An Essay upon Study, wherein Directions are given for the Due Conduct thereof, and the Collection of a Library, proper for the purpose consisting of the Choicest books in all the several Parts of Learning. by John Clarke,* published in 1731.

APPENDIX

The Catalogue

The books, with the exception of the Blazeby Collection, are in sections corresponding, in the main, to the divisions in the Subject Catalogue. The Passage contains books on Travel, Hymnology, Liturgies, Education, Science, and the Periodicals. Cards relating to books in the Passage are marked " P," and those relating to books in the Gallery are marked " G." The Blazeby Collection, in accordance with the terms of the bequest, are separated from the rest in two blocks: (1) Biography and Literature; (2) History, Theology, and Miscellaneous. All bear a Blazeby stamp on the title-page, and the corresponding cards in the Catalogue are marked " Blazeby." The Prints, etc., belonging to the Collection are kept in one of the cupboards under lock and key. In another cupboard are the first editions of value and all MSS., except those in the showcase and a set of Nonconformist academy lectures in the Gallery.

All books bear the stamp of the College on the title-page, and on the inside cover of Dictionaries, Encyclopædias, and works of reference a printed slip is attached indicating that they are not to be taken out of the Library. Collected works of authors have been kept together on the ground floor and in the Gallery. Other exceptions to the shelf classification are due (*a*) to the need, for reasons of economy in space, to keep together books belonging to a series, and (*b*) to the size of the volumes and of the shelves.

Duplicates have been kept only where they are bound up with other pamphlets or sermons.

All books, tracts, pamphlets, sermons, etc., are catalogued in duplicate on typewritten cards, the shelf letter and number being written in pencil so as to be easily erased, if it become necessary to remove books from their present position. The Catalogues are (*a*) A Classified Subject Catalogue; (*b*) An Authors' Catalogue.

In the Subject Catalogue each main subject (with its sub-divisions) follows in alphabetical order, the names of authors being in the same order, and the works of each author being arranged according to date.

In the Authors' Catalogue, all the works of each author are on one or more cards; the title being given in brief with place and date of publication. Added to the list of works is a list of the biographies of the author, or of works bearings on his writings. The name of the author is printed in capitals and birth and death dates given, wherever possible. Authors of works published anonymously are named, and editors of composite works, dictionaries, etc.

Each card in the Subject Catalogue contains a copy of the title-page, occasionally abbreviated, the type of volume, place and date of publication, pagination, and, where given, the edition. In works of more than two volumes, pagination is omitted. Of all anonymous works, the first word (excluding the articles) is given. Of rare and valuable works, the printer's name is added, and bibliographical details inserted, together with references to MS. notes included in the books. First editions of importance are noted as such. All particulars known, but not printed on the title-page, are enclosed in brackets.

The card catalogue of seventeenth and eighteenth century Unitarian Tracts in Dr. Williams' Library was used in compiling, comparing, and completing the cards for the similar department in the Summerville collection. In bound volumes of tracts and sermons, names of authors and works are written on the leaf before the first title-page. The printed collection of Arber's Reprints, prepared by Thomas Seccombe for the John Rylands Library, was cut up, and each entry pasted on a card, affording a detailed index to this valuable collection of Tudor and seventeenth century writings, edited by Edward Arber.

Biographical works are entered under the names of the persons biographised in the Subject Catalogue, and under the names of the writers of the books in the Authors' Catalogue. Cards are included in the former catalogue for all lives prefixed to collected works, or forming part of memorial sermons and pamphlets. Dictionaries of biography and volumes of collected biographical studies are separately classified, and the separate lives in the latter are also catalogued under the appropriate letter in the main biographical section.

In the classical section of the Subject Catalogue, the Anglicised form of authors' names has been adopted, and, similarly, in the Patristic section, the English names of fathers have been used.

In the Authors' Catalogue, classical works are included under the names of the classical writers and also under those of the editors of the texts.

Articles in the Bulletin of the *John Rylands Library*, the *Transactions of the Unitarian Historical Society*, the *Oxford Tracts for the Times*, and a few other similar publications are separately catalogued in both Authors' and Subject Catalogues.

Memorial sermons are catalogued under the names of the preachers and again under those of the departed.

Unitarian Chapel Histories are catalogued in the Subject Catalogue both under the names of the chapels and those of the authors.

Framed portraits, engravings and photographs in the House (excepting those of students in the common-room) are catalogued in the subject Catalogue.

Cross references in the catalogue will enable readers consulting the works of an author to learn almost all that the Library contains relative to the subject of their quest.

INDEX

Made in the USA
San Bernardino, CA
13 May 2014